GOODREADS FOR AUTHORS

GOODREADS FOR AUTHORS

How To Promote Your Books With Goodreads

Michelle Campbell-Scott

Praise For *Goodreads For Authors*

"An easy-to-use, informative, step-by-step guide for all authors, especially new ones, seeking to use Goodreads as a valued marketing tool."

> ~ **Cheryl Kaye Tardif**, International bestselling author of *How I Made Over $42,000 In 1 Month Selling My Kindle eBooks*

"As a fulltime author of more than 15 books, I've spent considerable time investigating new ways to promote my books. Over the last several months I've read several articles about the value of Goodreads but never took the time to dig into the system.

When I received an advance review copy of Michelle Campbell-Scott's new book, Goodreads for Authors, I realized what a tremendous marketing opportunity I'd been missing. Not only is Goodreads easy to set up, it allows authors like me to reach niche audiences in a way few other marketing venues do.

Authors are frequently torn about how best to spend their marketing vs. their writing time; after reading this book I know that Goodreads will be among my top marketing strategies."

> ~ **Nancy Hendrickson**, author of *How to Write for Kindle* & *Writer's Block Vanquished!*

"Yesterday I walked around a corner and discovered a whole new world, a parallel universe for book lovers and authors. Michelle Campbell-Scott's 'Goodreads for Authors' introduced me to Goodreads and within an hour of starting her book I had a new profile, more than 200 friends on this powerful platform, and had rated 91 books. At the end of two hours, while still reading the step-by-step instructions in the book, I had applied for an author profile. Two hours - that's how fast and easy it is to get started with this vast platform of potential for authors new and established if you allow yourself to be guided by 'Goodreads for Authors'.

Michelle's comprehensive work isn't just an introduction to Goodreads. She takes you beyond the front door and shows you the major spaces and places inside, including some of the charming nooks and crannies. Not only can 'Goodreads for Authors' serve as a beginners' guide, it can also help you plan a strategy for gradual escalation of your involvement with Goodreads with the end of improving your marketing (and sales) as well as having a fine time with other bookish folk.

Clearly Michelle's expertise in social media comes into play as she cautions and instructs on the best uses of Goodreads by authors. I got the message: don't barge into the room and holler, "Hey, who wants to buy my stuff?" She blends line by line instruction with thoughtful explanations of why this book-lovers oasis is constructed and run as it is.

You certainly can noodle around Goodreads on your own and figure it out, sort of like you maybe did with Facebook, sorta kinda getting it over time. Alternatively you can just buy 'Goodreads for Authors', get up to speed quickly, and start planning your next and future strategic book marketing steps."

> ~ **Bruce Brown**, Health & Fitness coach and author, www.beingbrucebrown.com

"I have spent hours that I will never get back trying to figure out how to use the Goodreads site effectively as an author. And, while I did make some progress, I had no idea what I was doing, or what was important to do, or why. I am thrilled that someone, finally, has written this guide. I learned so much in such a short time!

In fact, before I even finished this book, I had imported my blog feed into my author profile blog (simply by following the author's instructions - I had no idea what I was doing) and it worked. I plan to re-visit this book again and again and highly recommend it for every author (except authors in my category!)."

~ **Donna Smallin Kuper**, organizing expert & author

"It's no secret that there are thousands of ways to market a book. It is also no secret that the job of marketing falls on the author nowadays. How in the world can busy authors keep up?

One answer is to get some help (or maybe a lot of help) and this book is one way to do it. Goodreads.com is just one of the many social media platforms authors can use to reach their audience and, like the rest, it has a learning curve. You can try to figure it all out on your own, but if you'd prefer some help and to shorten the curve, 'Goodreads for Authors' has exactly what you need.

The book is well put together in an easy to navigate, logical order that is useful for beginners to intermediate social media users. Author Michelle Campbell-Scott includes a broad view of what you need to know, as well as a ton of little details that make this a truly comprehensive soup to nuts book.

If you're an author and you've considered learning to use Goodreads to connect with your audience, you cannot go wrong if you choose this book as your guide.

~ *Cheryl Pickett*, nonfiction publishing consultant and author of *Creation Inspirations: A New View of the World Around You*

"Being a self-published author myself and having to promote as well as market my own books – it's part of your underlying success or (hopefully not) failure of any book as a self-published author. Soon after I published my first book on Amazon Kindle, one of the first things that happened was I got invited to Goodreads. Being a complete stranger to self-publishing at the time, I didn't have the smallest of clues as to what or why I'd be spending my time on Goodreads.

I was honored to receive a review copy of 'Goodreads for Authors' and the first thing that caught my interest about the author's book was in fact the title. Some will call it fate; I choose to call it destiny... it turns out at the time of this book's publication I had just published the latest and third installment of my first series of books on Amazon Kindle. I needed to come up with new marketing ideas for my books, and fast as well.

The first chapter encouraged me to get out of my comfort zone and take the time to update my Goodreads profile so I can start tapping into the many advantages of being an active member on the platform. The author outlined the first steps of getting your Goodreads profile set up and she also lists the many different ways to take care of various tasks as a self-published author on Goodreads.

The rest of the book is written and structured with the same goal in mind: to engage the reader with detailed, step-by-step explanations and instructions to follow in order to get each aspect within Goodreads mastered and optimized according to its full potential.

If you are tied to a tight schedule as I am, you are going to find the "in a hurry" section at the end of some chapters to be true genius. As the name suggests, it is a quick overview of the key take-away elements of each chapter, which comes in handy when you are in a hurry, perfect for quick reference, and a check-list during and after implementation. I can honestly write a whole book on the magnificent value this detailed book will provide you on getting started as an active self-published author marketing your books on Goodreads.

Excellent value, detailed encouragement throughout with even the occasional glimpse of humor – quite the exciting combination for an instructional guide."

~ **Ruan Oosthuizen**, author of the *Birth of a Freelance Blogger* series

You can download images, charts, and book bonuses at the following link (no signup required):

http://www.forauthors.info/goodreads-for-authors-book-downloads

Use the password: **GR4AbookBonuses**

PLEASE NOTE:

Goodreads is a rapidly growing and developing site. Therefore the screenshots in this book may not be exactly the same as the screen when you go to Goodreads. I keep the book as up-to-date as possible but sometimes people bring new features to my attention that I haven't come across before - or the fact that some things have been removed.

If you come across substantial differences, I would be very grateful if you would let me know what they are, so I can help other authors stay up-to-date.

Find me on Goodreads or via the contact page on my website **www.forauthors.info**

I post news of updates and changes to the Goodreads platform on the ForAuthors site.

*For Kat, who has inspired and encouraged
my writing since the day she was born.*

"The author's job is to write a great book and to keep his readers engaged and interested while he writes the next one."

~ Otis Chandler, Founder & CEO of Goodreads

ॐ ॐ

"You reap what you sow. The beauty of Goodreads is that you know you're sowing in a field where everyone, by definition and self-selection, loves to read."

~ Guy Kawasaki, co-author of *APE*

CONTENTS

FOREWORD

By Tom Oberbichler Author, writer's coach & NLP trainer

LITTLE DID I KNOW, when I met Michelle in a Facebook group for self-published authors, that it would be she who would fulfill such a need for us. Being an independent and self-published author and writer myself, I share one great need with my fellow authors: I want to connect with readers.

I love writing and publishing books. I write How to/Advice books focusing on emotional success and self-publishing and, once the book is written, I not only want others to become my readers, I am always looking for ways to connect with people who have read my books, to get their views and share their experiences. Some of this I get through my blog and Facebook but I am constantly on the look-out for new opportunities - and then I literally 'Stumbled Upon' Goodreads.

I have been fascinated by the seemingly infinite possibilities Goodreads offers to readers and authors alike and I like the easy way to use them which Michelle shows in her book.

There is only so much time each day and between writing, formatting, publishing, and marketing your books, it can be trying to squeeze in time to explore a new field.

And new social networks seem to pop up each week! Keeping your focus can be challenging.

Goodreads, though, isn't just another social network. Goodreads focuses on books and they are at the center of everything. And we do love books, don't we? Every successful author is an avid reader first – in my world.

So I am very grateful to Michelle for having undertaken the effort to thoroughly explore all the options Goodreads offers and to transform all the information mixed with her personal experiences into this comprehensive book 'Goodreads for Authors'.

Aside from the general overview, I really appreciate Michelle's approach. In the well structured chapters of her book Michelle provides you an extensive step-by-step process and guides you through all the features waiting for you. This may be a bit time consuming but, when you have done it once, you will benefit from it for a long time.

Michelle also offers the other, the quick approach. At the end of many chapters she has included a quick summary which you can read 'if you're in a hurry'.

If you are an author, a writer or want to be one, you will get a lot of value out of this guide, which actually represents a shortcut for you not only to use Goodreads to promote your books but to benefit from participating in the activity on the site. Some of the beneficial things you can learn in this book:

- ❖ Find groups to meet other authors, as well as readers, for specific genres.
- ❖ Meet other people who love books.
- ❖ Create successful giveaways of the hard copy edition of your book.
- ❖ Promote your free days and other promotions with events.
- ❖ Share and exchange your own reading experiences.
- ❖ Get your books read and reviewed.
- ❖ Get to know other interesting books.
- ❖ Learn how bestselling authors use Goodreads to promote their books.

With your engagement on Goodreads, you can notice increased exposure, reviews and sales of your books, while having met and connected with lots of like minded folks. Thank you Michelle for having opened up this lane for us.

After working hard to study this book and optimize your presence on Goodreads, I suggest you put your feet up and read Michelle's book, *Mo, the Talking Dog*. You're in for a pleasure read, because Michelle knows how to tell a story.

To your success and fun.

be wonderful!

Thomas "Tom" Oberbichler

PREFACE

❦

Don't fall into the trap of thinking of Goodreads as just another place to have a presence as an author. Think of it as a place to talk about books. If you do, one day your Goodreads friends could be talking about your books.

~ Michelle Campbell-Scott

I HADN'T HEARD OF GOODREADS until a friend's status popped up on my Facebook news stream to say she had just finished reading a book and had written a review of it on Goodreads. The friend is a well-read former librarian who, like me, loves history so I clicked on the link to read her review. It was about Eric Ives's biography of the short-lived English Tudor Queen, Anne Boleyn. Straight after reading her review, I ordered the book.

I could stop there, really, couldn't I?!

As authors, we want to find ways of getting our books in front of potential readers and we want them to be able to buy them quickly and easily. Amazon helps that, of course, but it only goes so far. Amazon is a massive catalogue and does an excellent job of cross-selling books. If you look at one book it will come up with suggestions of others you may like. It tries really hard to make itself very individual to the reader but actually it is quite impersonal because the biggest failing of Amazon is that you can't make relationships on there.

You can on Goodreads. I bought that book because:

❖ My friend uses Goodreads.

- ❖ I like her and respect her views.
- ❖ I was able to quickly and easily find and read her review, then …
- ❖ Buy the book within a few seconds.

I can browse my other friends' Goodreads bookshelves to see what they are reading/have read and, often, I go ahead and buy some of those books myself. That's because our friends will often have similar interests to us.

For example, my fiancé is an archer, he shoots at a local field archery club. In the UK we don't hunt animals, we use targets, so that fits in with my beliefs and I joined his club about a year ago. I LOVE it! I have finally found a sport I can do. You don't have to run about and get sweaty, you just stand there and point your bow, it's great!

I wanted to get better at archery and did what most compulsive readers do, searched Amazon for suitable books. There were quite a few, so I read the reviews and chose one. It was a bit of a disappointment. I asked at the club and often people had favorite archery books but couldn't remember the titles or authors.

As these things go, over time you start to make deeper relationships, swap telephone numbers, add each other on Facebook, etc. Via Facebook, I found that some of the people in the club were also on Goodreads (mainly women, interestingly) and was able to pick out the archery books on their virtual shelves!

Sometimes they had written reviews, sometimes not; but I was able to see which books they had read and we enjoyed chatting about them. Those chats meant that I bought a few more books. Amazon couldn't do that for me. It could only serve up reviews written by strangers, not all of them actually doing archery, certainly not all at my beginner level, not all the field type (there is also target archery, which doesn't interest me, you don't get to go play in the woods) and often the books included unsavory (to me) advice about how to butcher any animals you manage to shoot.

Goodreads was much more helpful, more targeted (no pun intended!) and felt more personal. I started to realize the power of it as a reader.

I didn't think of using Goodreads as an author – indeed I didn't know it was possible – until earlier this year. An author friend I respect has a presence on Goodreads and advised me to do the same.

I am in a number of author groups on Facebook and LinkedIn. I 'Liked' the Facebook Goodreads page and was astonished that only one of my author friends had [then] also liked the page. He happens to be a very successful author who sells tons of books (Derek Olsen, best known for *The 4-Week Financial Turnaround*). Coincidence? No, I think part of his success is due to his activity on Goodreads.

It is slightly more fiddly to sign up as an author, but I did so and linked my profile to the two books I had available on Amazon for Kindles.

I started getting friend requests from other people on Goodreads and I added some books to my virtual 'Read' and 'To Read' shelves but that was pretty much it.

I had no idea how to use Goodreads to promote my books or interact with my readers and potential readers and I didn't know anyone who could tell me how.

I did notice, though, that a few of the authors I follow on Twitter have Goodreads accounts and often mention them on Twitter.

I also noticed that people would occasionally run events on Goodreads. When I asked them about them they had generally either been told how to do it by a friend or had learned the hard, long way.

No-one knew of a book, course, or guide that covered how to use Goodreads as an author.

Indie (independent) authors don't tend to have much spare time. As well as writing, we have to do all the marketing jobs that traditional publishers do for their clients. We need to divide our week into writing time and marketing time and there isn't much left to devote to learning.

So I didn't get around to discovering how to use Goodreads to promote my books and it niggled away at the back of my mind that I should find out more about it.

My daughter was between jobs recently. She does modeling and acting and often works part-time in a local bookstore when she's home so she has her finger somewhat on the pulse of the publishing industry. I put her to work doing research with me before I started writing this book.

We set ourselves the task of finding out how best to use Goodreads as reader initially, then we looked at how successful authors were using the platform.

We started by following the authors she knew were popular, to see how they (or their publishers) were managing their Goodreads profiles.

We learnt how to create an interesting profile, make the most of the features Goodreads offers authors, interact with others, build relationships, promote books and integrate other social networking platforms.

The more I learned about Goodreads, the more astonished I was at the power of the thing! The features are amazing and not many authors are making the most of them. Those that are, of course, are in the thousands of dollars a month bracket.

Fiction authors tend to be the ones who make the news, the ones who earn millions. Of course, we all know that those are the rarities, that's why they make the news. Most of us earn a 'normal' wage, many unfortunately earn just a little.

Nonfiction authors don't tend to make headlines that shout about massive earnings and six-figure traditional publishing contracts. That doesn't mean they aren't selling lots of books. I know of several who are earning eye-watering sums of money, they just don't shout about it!

I read a lot of nonfiction and find that Goodreads is as good for nonfiction books as it is for fiction. Both are picked by book club groups and there are lots of nonfiction genres on Goodreads, e.g. biography, business, cookbooks, etc. You can add your own genres too.

I decided to make the knowledge I gained about Goodreads available for other authors, as I hadn't found anything of its like to help me when I was trying to find out how best to use Goodreads.

A little time on Goodreads will unearth plenty of authors to follow, so you can see for yourself what they do to keep their readers engaged. One in particular is worth a mention now – in case you need convincing of the need to establish a author Goodreads profile and routine.

Cheryl Kaye Tardif came onto my radar for two reasons:

❖ She wrote a book called *How I Made Over $42,000 In 1 Month Selling My Kindle eBooks*. A title like that kind of captures your attention when you're a Kindle author.

❖ She is Canadian. My Dad was an engineer for the Canadian Pacific shipping line and it left him with a deep and abiding love for Canada in general, and Canadians in particular. I grew up with stories of the wonders of the land across the water (I'm from the UK). I'm fascinated by the place and by the people.

I followed Cheryl (I can call her that – she's a Goodreads friend, it's a friendly place!) on Goodreads. She's very good at what she does – both writing (page-turning thrillers) and marketing (bank-pleasing royalties).

I asked her for her thoughts on Goodreads and this is what she said:

> *"Goodreads and other library/book collection social networks are vital to connecting authors with readers, and it's a must-have for any writer looking at a career in this industry."*

Cheryl uses Goodreads intelligently, she obviously has it high up her list of profitable marketing tactics. She currently has 3,564 friends and nearly 500 books on her shelves (Goodreads shelves are populated with books read, books to read, and books currently reading – so that doesn't mean she has written 500 books!).

She has populated her author profile with a blog, events and videos, she comments in groups and on discussions, and she updates her status regularly.

This is a highly successful author. If she is doing it, it is probably worth doing.

Readers are always looking for new authors and authors find it hard to get their book in front of potential readers because the marketplace is very crowded. Goodreads is the place for the two to meet.

That's even more true since Amazon bought Goodreads. They acquired the site at the end of March 2013. Authors have reported seeing Goodreads reviews on their Amazon book pages. The Amazon buyout could be seen as a big organization getting even bigger and monopolizing part of the publishing industry. Or it could be seen as an author's dream – the biggest site in the world for book sales marrying the biggest site in the world for readers.

Whatever your feelings, it is clear that authors can only benefit from having a lively presence on Goodreads.

I hope you find this an interesting and useful read.

Michelle

PREFACE
IF YOU'RE IN A HURRY

- ❖ Goodreads is much more personalized than Amazon and other sales sites.
- ❖ People are more likely to buy books that their friends have recommended than those strangers have recommended.
- ❖ You can have an author profile on Goodreads and use it to promote your own books.
- ❖ Highly successful authors spend time on Goodreads.

WHY YOU NEED
TO READ THIS BOOK

❧❧

THIS BOOK WILL BENEFIT you – hopefully tremendously – if you are an author *and* a reader. There are numerous ways to promote your book(s) on Goodreads but the most important, long-lasting way is to be a reader, and to chat to people about books.

I have written the chapters in the order that you need to do things on Goodreads – starting with joining as a user, then converting that profile into an author profile, learning about bookshelves and groups, and going on to the various ways to promote your book.

This book will help you if you:

- ❖ Joined Goodreads but don't know what to do on the site (see Section One).
- ❖ Need a way to find more readers (see Sections One and Two).
- ❖ Want to learn from other authors (see the Groups chapter).
- ❖ Need a way of advertising your books but have been disappointed with the performance (and the price!) of Google AdWords or Facebook ads (see the Advertising chapter).
- ❖ Have a limited or non-existent budget and need to promote your books, urgently! (see the Giveaway Promotions chapter and the Promote Free eBooks chapter).

This book may not be as much benefit to you if you:

- ❖ Are a talented Internet Marketer who is writing (or outsourcing the writing of) books to make a profit and you will probably move on to the next thing (e.g. video marketing) sooner or later.
- ❖ Don't have the time to learn how Goodreads works.
- ❖ Aren't a reader and don't enjoy discussing books with other readers.

Goodreads is, first and foremost, for readers. Readers who love books.

It is therefore the very best place to be for the author who is in it for the long-term, who seeks to connect with and engage his/her readers and build lasting relationships.

If that describes you, read on!

SECTION ONE

GET TO KNOW GOODREADS QUICKLY

I F YOU ARE TEMPTED to skip over this section and get to the juicy stuff about how to promote your book, please don't. You'll be wasting your time. If you attempted to write a book on a computer without ever having used a computer, you would be in for a frustrating and lengthy time. You would probably end up smashing in the computer screen and throwing the keyboard out of the window after a fruitless search for the mysterious 'Any' key.

Goodreads is a big site but, if you are willing to invest a little time to go through the steps outlined in this book, you will 'get it' and it will become familiar and enjoyable very quickly.

I've kept the chapters as short as possible but some are more lengthy than others as they contain step-by-step instructions. I estimate that it will take you about an hour to get familiar and comfortable with Goodreads using Section One of this book.

An hour. Worth it? You bet.

Then you can use Section Two to learn how to promote your book(s), dipping in and out of it at your leisure.

Section Three includes optional extras such as handy widgets and mobile apps.

I've set the chapters up as the steps you need to take so, if you can, work through them one by one.

These are the initial steps and approximate timings for Section One, where you sign up and get to know Goodreads:

- ❖ Sign up as a Goodreads user – <5 minutes.
- ❖ Get to know the Goodreads dashboard – <5 minutes.
- ❖ Convert your user account into an author account – 5-10 minutes (plus a bit of waiting time for your request to be approved).
- ❖ Learn about profiles, improve your profile – 10 minutes.
- ❖ Learn about bookshelves, add books to your shelves – 5-10 minutes.
- ❖ Make some friends – 10 minutes.
- ❖ Learn about groups, join some and participate – 10 minutes.
- ❖ Find out about recommendations – 5 minutes.

Going by my beta readers, you could add up to another hour to really make an impact - put photos and videos on your profile, beef up your blog, find & add friends and shelve lots of books.

This can be as long or as short a task as you want (you can do it gradually, over time). Goodreads gives you back what you put into it.

This could be the very thing that your writing career needs to take you to the next level of success. I'm so excited to be able to share in that with you.

Let's go and get stuck in!

CHAPTER 1

GOODREADS OVERVIEW

GOODREADS CALLS ITSELF: "The largest site for readers and book recommendations in the world." It certainly is large, with over 1.3 billion books listed and 50 million reviews (April 2016). It is a huge site – you will keep finding new things even after using it for a few years!

Their membership doubled in the year from 2011 to 2012, from 6.5 million users in 2011 to 13 million in 2012. It reached 25 million users in 2014 and is currently at 40 million and rising.

It is larger than Shelfari and LibraryThing (two other, smaller book cataloguing sites) combined.

The idea is for users to list the books they are reading, have read, and want to read, so that they can recommend them to others.

It is more than just a book recommendation site though. It is possible to form book clubs (with people from all over the world, which is pretty cool - imagine discussing *Wild Swans* with people in China!), write & read reviews of books and compare books with others. There are now over 20 million reviews on Goodreads.

The site was founded in 2007 by Otis Y Chandler, a software engineer, and Elizabeth Khuri Chandler, a journalist and editor. They are very active on the site and it is possible to friend both of them.

Otis – the great-great-great-grandson of the founder of the Los Angeles Times - had noticed that he loved looking at his friends' bookshelves to see what they had read (I'm with him on that!). He thought it would be a great idea to create a site with virtual bookshelves so people could not only see their friends' bookshelves but also find out what they thought about all the books they had read.

The result is a very comprehensive, easy-to-navigate site that is rapidly growing in popularity – both among readers and authors.

HOW IT IS SIMILAR TO FACEBOOK

If you are familiar with Facebook you should be able to get used to Goodreads very quickly.

Facebook profile = Goodreads user profile

Facebook page = Goodreads author profile

Facebook friends = Goodreads friends

Facebook page fans = Goodreads author fans

If you aren't familiar with Facebook it doesn't matter – you can get started on Goodreads quickly and easily without a huge learning curve, just by following the instructions in this book. Goodreads says that Facebook and Twitter aren't the most popular places for people to find new books, and the statistics support that.

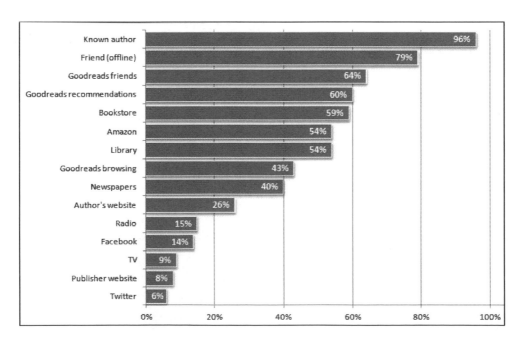

Where people discover new books. Source: The Goodreads Blog.

Only 6% of people claim to have discovered new books on Twitter and just 14% on Facebook.

HOW IT DIFFERS FROM AMAZON

Authors know that reviews sell books. Goodreads is full of reviews but you can also write reviews on Amazon, so why would you choose Goodreads?

There are some very compelling reasons:

❖ It is easier to follow reviewers on Goodreads. There are no alerts on Amazon. If you read a fantastic review of a book, then read and love the book yourself, you are more likely to want to follow that reviewer's other reviews on Goodreads. It makes sense – you don't waste money on books you aren't going to enjoy. There is a way to follow Amazon reviewers but it isn't obvious. It is also less useful as not all Amazon reviewers stick to one genre or style. You are more likely to find good Goodreads reviewers who specialize in the type of reading you like.

❖ Goodreads will notify you when reviewers you like post new reviews.

❖ Goodreads works as a social network – Amazon is purely a sales site. Goodreads is a sort of Facebook for literary-minded people. You get to make relationships, discuss books, discover others. Amazon is more of an impersonal shop window.

❖ On Goodreads, you can display the books you have read on a virtual shelf and allow others to explore them.

For authors, having a presence on Goodreads is an excellent idea. You are able to find out what people are currently reading and enjoying, what's popular, which authors have good followings, how the bestselling authors are interacting with their readers, and much more.

Once you start making friends on Goodreads, you can make relationships, build trust, and write reviews. You will naturally gain a following and those people are much more likely to buy your own books – then review them.

As in business, people buy from people. We are all more likely to read a book if a trusted/similarly-minded friend recommends it. *So getting on Goodreads and making friends is the most important first step.*

There are other, more powerful reasons that you should consider being on Goodreads, though – as well as spending both time and money on the site:

❖ CBS News reported that part of the explanation for the popularity of *Fifty Shades of Grey* was because of Goodreads.

❖ Publishers take notice of Goodreads. Berkley bought *Bared to You* (a *Fifty Shades of Grey*-type novel) and cited its 2,500 reviews on Goodreads as a major reason.

❖ Users visit the site frequently (one statistic says more than twice per day) and spend 4.4 minutes per visit.

❖ Every day, there are thousands of reviews written, book recommendations sent, giveaways entered and authors 'fanned'. Every time someone does something with a book – shelves it, rates it, reviews it, comments on it – it shows up in their friends' [Goodreads] feeds and possibly on their own social media profiles.

❖ The average active Goodreads user has shelved 54 books, written 10 reviews, has 35 friends, and has 19 books on their To Read shelf.

❖ The community includes readers, booksellers, librarians, book bloggers, teachers, and authors..

❖ 21% of all Goodreads users have a BOOK BLOG. Is your author antenna standing to attention? Mine was when I read that the first time.

OVERVIEW
IF YOU'RE IN A HURRY

❖ Goodreads is social – not sales. Social sells because it is relationship-based and people find it more trustworthy.

❖ You can browse the bookshelves of other authors, potential buyers and existing readers.

❖ Establishing an author profile on Goodreads gives you more access to potential readers.

❖ Goodreads can propel your book into viral-type popularity.

❖ You can do valuable, informal market research by seeing what the current and forthcoming trends are by participating on Goodreads.

CHAPTER 2

THE GOODREADS DASHBOARD

THIS IS A QUICK run-through of the main features of Goodreads, so you don't have to waste hours clicking around trying to find everything.

Log in quickly - Using one of your other social media profiles is the quickest way to log into Goodreads – even on a smartphone. I generally use Facebook.

When you log in you will be taken to the Goodreads home page – which is dynamic (i.e. ever changing) and tailored to you. It will be populated according to your reading and Goodreads habits.

At the very top you should see the Goodreads main navigation. This navigation bar will be there wherever you are in the site – so it is quick and easy to get to anywhere else. Anywhere you need to go on the site can be reached from this bar or from the dropdowns next to Browse, Community, and your profile picture thumbnail.

Figure 1 - the 2016 navigation bar

The word **'goodreads'** on the left - a clickable link to take you back to your home page.

HOME – back to the main page.

MY BOOKS – takes you to your bookshelves.

BROWSE – which leads to:

- ❖ Recommendations
- ❖ Choice Awards
- ❖ Giveaways
- ❖ New Releases
- ❖ Lists
- ❖ News & Interviews
- ❖ Explore

COMMUNITY – which leads to:

- ❖ Groups
- ❖ Quotes
- ❖ Ask the Author
- ❖ Trivia
- ❖ Quizzes
- ❖ Creative Writing
- ❖ People
- ❖ Events

A **SEARCH** box – type in this to find a book or author, using the book's title, ISBN, or the author's name. Goodreads isn't like Google, it doesn't try to guess what you mean if you spell something incorrectly, so you need to ensure you have the exact spelling.

- ❖ On the right-hand side of the screen, you should see:

BELL icon – notifications about your Goodreads activity.

ENVELOPE icon – messages other Goodreads users have sent you.

FRIENDS icon – a page with all your Goodreads friends. Go here to check out their profiles and bookshelves, and to send them messages.

PROFILE PICTURE thumbnail –a DROPDOWN appears when you hover over your profile picture thumbnail, with useful links to:

- ❖ View Profile
- ❖ Author Dashboard
- ❖ Friends

❖ My Quotes

❖ My Comments

❖ My Groups

❖ My Reading Challenge

❖ My Favorite Genres

❖ Friends' Recommendations

❖ Account Settings

❖ Help

❖ Sign out

As you can see, Goodreads gives us multiple ways to get to different pages, so we can easily get to where we want to be. The new layout is a big improvement on the old one.

THE DASHBOARD
IF YOU'RE IN A HURRY

❖ The top navigation bar will be displayed on every page in the entire Goodreads site, with the exception of the Self-Serve Advertising area. If you're in the advertising area, go to **www.goodreads.com** again to get the navigation bar back.

❖ The Home page will contain updates from friends and groups you are in, your own information (profile link, number of books you have rated, currently reading, your bookshelves, etc.), etc.

❖ You can get anywhere on Goodreads from the top navigation bar, use the dropdown menus to find other areas.

CHAPTER 3

SIGN UP AS A READER

YOU HAVE TO SIGN up for Goodreads as a reader before you can sign up as an author. Again, this is similar to Facebook, where you need to have a personal profile before you can create a page. It is a lot less fiddly than Facebook, though, you don't have to mess about logging in as different pages, you're just you wherever you are on Goodreads.

Signing up as a reader is quick and easy – you want to encourage all your friends and family to do so ... and the mailman ... and anyone you meet in an elevator ... and get them to put the books you have written on their shelves.

Signing up as an author takes a little longer as you need to:

❖ Have a book published
❖ Request an author profile

The first step, though, is to sign up as a reader. We'll cover signing up as an author in the next chapter.

STEP ONE – SIGN UP

Go to **www.goodreads.com** and click the SIGN UP button.

Enter your name, email address, a password, and click 'Sign up'. You could also click one of the social links – Facebook, Twitter or Google – and Goodreads will ask if you would like to set up an account with them. They're so polite!

Click CREATE A NEW ACCOUNT.

If you use one of the social platforms to sign up, you will be notified if any contacts from that platform are on Goodreads. They automatically make existing friends Goodreads friends (a little cheeky!) but you can deselect the checkbox to prevent them from doing that in future if any existing friends join Goodreads. You might not want to do that though – the more contacts on Goodreads the better.

Click CONTINUE.

STEP TWO – FIND CONTACTS (OPTIONAL)

You will then see a screen asking if you want Goodreads to search to see if any of your contacts from other areas of your life are on Goodreads (Gmail, Facebook, Yahoo, Hotmail or Twitter).

You can click on these to find them, or click 'Skip This Step'.

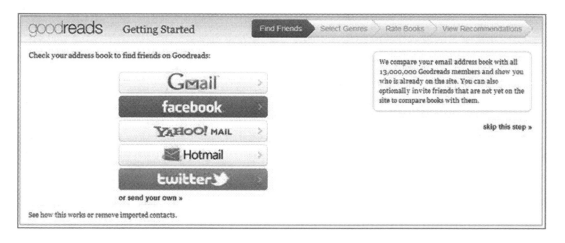

There have been privacy issues with Facebook apps in the past, they are one way hackers can sneak into your account. Having a good password policy helps this but it's ultimately your call about whether you want to use Facebook apps.

Personally I do use the Goodreads one because I feel its usefulness outweighs any danger. It is very easy to remove an app if it ever gives you cause for concern though.

So you would click LOG IN WITH FACEBOOK and allow Goodreads to search your Facebook contacts to see if any of them are on Goodreads. Goodreads doesn't have access to your Facebook password, it is only able to search your contacts because you have logged in.

Let's skip this step for now – and this is a good idea, as it gives you chance to set up your presence on Goodreads before starting to connect with people.

Click SKIP THIS STEP or I DON'T WANT TO ADD ANY MORE FRIENDS on the right-hand side.

STEP THREE – SELECT GENRES

[OPTIONAL BUT ADVISABLE]

This step can be skipped but there's no harm in selecting your genres now. Click the checkboxes next to the genres you like to read – you can choose as many as you want to. If your favorite genre isn't listed, click DON'T SEE YOUR FAVORITE GENRES HERE? [not shown], which will allow you to type in a genre and search for it.

STEP FOUR – RATE BOOKS THAT YOU'VE READ

[OPTIONAL BUT ADVISABLE]

This isn't compulsory – you can click I'M FINISHED RATING – but it is a good idea and it gets you into the swing of life on Goodreads.

The books that appear here are the very popular, highly reviewed ones. It will be a while before you will be able to get your books selected by Goodreads to appear here but it isn't impossible. Notice that they are generally well-known books, classics or by celebrities/mass-market authors.

You don't have to accept their suggestions, though. Click in the search box and type in the title of a book you have read.

I entered 'Let me call you sweetheart', one of Mary Higgins Clark's books. It brought up a list of possible matches – books with the same or similar titles, books by the same author. When you hover over the thumbnail images of the book covers, a popup will appear with some details. You can click on the book's title in that popup for even more information.

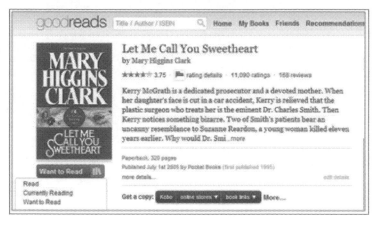

If you hover over the little green bookshelf below the book cover, next to the 'Want To Read' button, you will get the option of which of your shelves to put the book on.

'Read', 'Currently Reading' and 'Want To Read' are the default bookshelves, the one Goodreads automatically gives you when you sign up.

Click READ and the book will be added to your Read shelf, indicating to your Goodreads friends that you have read the book.

That will prompt Goodreads to ask you what you thought of it. This can be a one-click rating (click a star), or a longer, typed review.

Note that on the review screen you can choose whether or not to add your review to your update feed (which can be seen by your friends) and/or your Facebook page (if you have that enabled).

Write your review in the box. Check or uncheck the send to Facebook box, then click SAVE. When you have finished rating (click NEXT at the top of the page), Goodreads will take you to a Recommendations page.

If you have rated 20 or more books, this will be populated, if not don't worry, you can get to

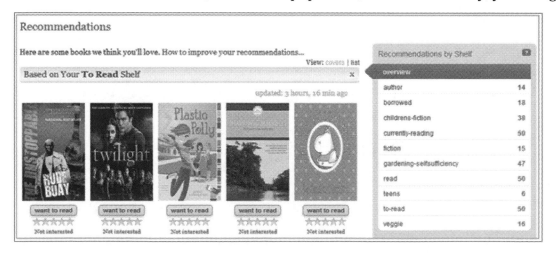

Recommendations any time from the main navigation bar.

If you signed up using Facebook, Twitter or Google, you may notice that you have a little profile picture at the top right of the Goodreads screen. If you click on that it will take you to your profile page.

If you don't have a profile picture it will be either because you don't have a profile picture on the platform you signed up with, or you signed up manually.

Either way, click on the little image or image placeholder at the top right-hand side of the Goodreads screen, which will take you to your profile page.

There won't be much information on there yet. You should have:

❖ A short profile at the top – with your profile picture and date of joining.

❖ Your bookshelves – everyone on Goodreads gets three standard bookshelves: Read; Currently Reading; To Read. You can add more as you go along.

❖ Some updates, if you rated any books during the sign-up process.

❖ Any friends that Goodreads imported for you from another social platform.

Once you are on Goodreads as a user (a reader), assuming you have a book already published you can go ahead and get an author profile.

Before you do, though, it is good to get to know Goodreads a little first. Otherwise, people may message you and you won't know how to respond. I know this because that is exactly what happened to me!

Once you have completed the sign up, you will need to respond to an email that Goodreads will send you, asking you to click a link to confirm that it was indeed you who signed up with them.

FINDING YOUR WAY AROUND

Goodreads generally adds some clickable suggestion boxes for newcomers. These contain the initial three things you need to do to get going on Goodreads:

❖ Add friends.[1]

❖ Rate [at least 20] books that you have read (in order to receive recommendations).

❖ Find/Add books.

---

[11] You may not be able to friend some people. There is a [current] limit of 5,000 friends.

You can click on those links and it is a good, quick way to get started. If they aren't there, use these:

- ❖ Add friends: www.goodreads.com/friend/invite
- ❖ Rate books: www.goodreads.com/user/rate_books
- ❖ Find/Add books by searching for them using the search box in the top navigation bar or go to: **www.goodreads.com/search**

Then add some to your 'To Read' shelf.

> **NOTE**: Occasionally, Goodreads goes a bit odd during registration and gets stuck at Step 2. You can just leave and come back again later, when it has had chance to calm down!

When you first join, your home page – which is dynamic and changes according to your use of the site – will be fairly empty. It soon fills up!

UPDATE YOUR PROFILE

Get to your profile from anywhere on Goodreads by scrolling up to the top of the page and clicking on your profile picture thumbnail at the top-right of the screen.

You can edit your profile from the profile page itself or by clicking the dropdown next to the profile picture thumbnail. Select EDIT PROFILE.

Complete the form to add details you want to share and click SAVE PROFILE SETTINGS at the bottom of the page.

SIGN UP
IF YOU'RE IN A HURRY

❖ Sign up for Goodreads and follow the steps.

❖ Click the confirmation link in the email Goodreads send.

❖ Add some friends (limit 5,000 per person).

❖ Select your favorite genres – be sure to include the genre (s) you write in.

❖ Rate books you've read. You need a minimum of 30. You don't need to write reviews for them, if you don't have time, just give them a star rating.

❖ Start finding your way around the site and do the initial 3 steps: Add friends; Rate books you've read; Find/add books to your To Read shelf.

CHAPTER 4

SIGN UP AS AN AUTHOR

CONVERTING YOUR USER PROFILE to an author profile sounds complicated but it isn't. All you have to do is 'claim' one of your books and provide some proof that you are the author. Before we look at how to do that, let's look at the difficult between user profiles and author profiles, so you'll know what you've got when you get it!

It officially takes Goodreads 2-3 business days to process sign-ups for authors. Most come through more quickly – about 24-36 hours. Use the time while waiting to get to know Goodreads as a reader, add lots of books to your shelves, join groups and start meeting people. It will not be wasted time.

User profiles and author profiles don't stand out as being different at first. For example, when you see the names of the members of a group, you can't immediately tell who is a user and who is an author. Click on their names, though, and it will become more obvious.

A user profile generally has buttons to:

- ❖ Add as a friend
- ❖ Send a message

It is sometimes possible to also recommend a book, compare books, and/or follow reviews – before you are connected – if the person hasn't set their profile as 'Private'. A lot of users do set their profiles to private though.

Once you are friends, you can select WRITE A STORY underneath the friend's profile, so you can let the world know how you know each other. I'm not sure why you would want to do this but the option is there!

An author profile has a BECOME A FAN button below the author's profile picture at the top left-hand side of the screen. There may also be links to:

❖ Add as a friend
❖ Follow reviews
❖ Send a message
❖ Compare books

Author profiles can contain many things, but not all authors populate their profiles. One of the big things you can do is have a blog – either pulled in from an outside source or a new Goodreads blog. We'll look at how those later on.

You may come across a few dead authors on the site! Oscar Wilde, for instance, has a profile. The only option on dead authors' profiles is the Become A Fan button – understandably!

The first process towards getting an author profile is to ...

Get Your Book Added To Goodreads

In the search box at the top of any Goodreads page, enter your book's name and click the magnifying glass. If your book appears in the results list:

❖ Click on it, then click on your author name.
❖ Scroll down and find the text IS THIS YOU? LET US KNOW. The 'let us know' bit is the hyperlink.
❖ On the next page, click to confirm that you are the author of that book, then type in a message asking to be added to the author program.
❖ If your book doesn't appear:
❖ You will get a No Results message.
❖ Underneath it, click the button STILL CAN'T FIND. There is also a MANUALLY ADD A BOOK link on most search pages.
❖ Enter the book's information and click CREATE at the bottom of the page. You can also now (since the Amazon buyout) add your cover by clicking BROWSE next to the ADD A COVER IMAGE FOR THIS BOOK line on the right-hand side of the page, and uploading your cover. Note that you can only do this once – if you

want to change the cover at a later stage you will need to put in a request in the Librarians Group.

❖ Authors can now add covers to their own books on Goodreads (since the Amazon buyout). Click the ADD COVER link on your book's page.

If you aren't already registered as a Goodreads author, you will receive an email when they have approved your request. It generally takes a day or two to arrive. Next time you log into Goodreads you will notice that you profile looks a little different and you have options you didn't have before, such as the ability to add videos and a blog.

ADD AN ADDITIONAL BOOK TO GOODREADS

If you already have a Kindle book listed on Goodreads and want to add the paperback version, go to your Kindle book's page and click MANUALLY ADD A BOOK. Then add the details. Click BROWSE next to ADD A COVER IMAGE FOR THIS BOOK, then search for and upload your cover.

CHANGING BOOK COVERS

We can add our own covers when we add our books to Goodreads but if you change your cover, you need to get a Librarian to update it..All you have to do is put in a request in the Librarians Group to ask a librarian to change it for you. We don't have the kind of database access that librarians do!

Add the following information to the post with a request for the new book cover to be added to the Goodreads catalogue:

❖ Title.
❖ Author(s) name(s).
❖ ISBN/ASIN.
❖ Publisher.
❖ Publication date.
❖ Format.
❖ Description.
❖ URL for a cover image on a site other than a sales site (not Amazon).

It is a good idea to provide ALL the information you can for your book. This gives more chances of it being found in a search.

Be sure to include the correct ISBN/ASIN and – importantly – include the page count. This allows readers to record their progress when they are reading your book, e.g. 'I'm on page 100 of 4000 of *War & Peace*'. It is in your best interests for them to be able to do that, you want readers' friends to see that they are reading your book.

Linking to your own cover image can be a problem if you don't have your own website or blog. If you do, upload the book cover as an image and get the URL (very easy if your site/blog is run on WordPress. Within WordPress click MEDIA > ADD MEDIA and upload the image. Then click on the live image and copy the URL from the address bar at the top of the page. Paste this into your post in the Librarians Group).

If you don't have a website/blog, you can use a site such as Flicker, which is a free photo sharing site. You can add photos and get a unique URL for each of them. It is possible to make them private, so they won't be listed by search engines and show up all over the Internet. You don't want to do that with your book covers though – you want them all over the Internet!

Sign up for Flickr then click UPLOAD at the top of the screen. You have the option to drag & drop photos or click to browse and choose photos. I upload 20-30 at a time, it doesn't take long.

Once your book cover image is uploaded you can click on it and get the unique URL.

Flickr currently has a 300MB upload limit per month before it asks you to upgrade to a paid Pro account - currently $6.95 per quarter.

ABOUT PEN NAMES

Goodreads doesn't have a way to handle pen names. What they suggest is to either:

- ❖ Have more than one author account, or
- ❖ Add your real name to your pen name when claiming your book, so it will be listed on your author profile.

There are many reasons for having pen names. With the explosion in popularity of the erotica genre, many people are finding a new love for writing adult tales! If they are also well-known for academic or literary books, they probably don't want both on their profiles.

Other people prefer to have one name associated with a particular genre because they have recognized expertise in that area. It is, of course, entirely possible to be an expert in more than one area – and many, many people are – but from the reader's point of view it could look like you aren't an expert because you have so many other things that you do. Unfair, perhaps, but it happens.

I use pen names because one of my genres is children's fiction and I don't want children and parents to have to wade through (eventually!) long lists of my nonfiction and historical fiction books to find suitable books for them.

On Amazon, pen names keep your books well apart, on Goodreads it is your call whether to use an additional author account in order to keep them separate.

AUTHOR SIGN UP
IF YOU'RE IN A HURRY

❖ Start with a standard Goodreads profile, then convert it to an author profile, either by selecting your name from the Goodreads database or by asking for your book to be added.

❖ Goodreads will then convert your user profile to an author profile. You will actually still have both. Your user profile details will show up when you are doing personal things on Goodreads, such as reviewing books and chatting to others. Your author profile will show up when other users find on your books and click on your name.

❖ Search for your books and claim them; otherwise add them manually and upload your cover.

❖ If your book is displaying an out-of-date cover – perhaps because it has been added by someone else, a while ago and you have since updated the cover – you will need to put a request in on the Librarians Group to ask for someone to replace the cover for you.

❖ Goodreads' suggestion: Create an 'Influences' shelf on your bookshelves. Add the books that have inspired you as a writer.

CHAPTER 5

SPRUCE UP YOUR PROFILE

IT IS IMPORTANT TO add lots of information to your profile, the more the better. Goodreads gives authors the opportunity to add a blog, videos, extended information, and other goodies.

Take advantage of them, they're all free.

PROFILE PICTURE

Your profile picture will follow your wherever you go on the Goodreads site. Get a good photo of yourself. It really is worth getting a professional shot done, it makes a huge difference.

I was first taught social media by a fantastic social media strategist, Liz Cable, who is Senior Lecturer in Digital & Social Media at Leeds Trinity University in Yorkshire, UK. Liz at that time was using a photograph (on Twitter, Facebook, and elsewhere) of herself outdoors, peeping around a tree. It was a beautiful and endearing photo that drew me to her (I'm a bit of a tree hugger myself!).

She told me that she would never use that photo on LinkedIn or other professional networking sites. She uses a business-like, professional head-and-shoulders shot. She explained that LinkedIn is a business platform and members (like authors on Goodreads) need to be seen to be professional, capable, and efficient. Not as someone you'd want to go on a hiking expedition with. Of course, if you write books about hiking that may be another matter! Even so, it is important to portray a professional image. You can add your hiking photos further down your profile page.

As authors we need to keep Liz's wisdom in mind. We need what Goodreads calls an 'authorial' photo to represent us on Goodreads, and elsewhere - online and off. Check out the book jackets of highly successful authors (I love Mary Higgins Clark's authorial photos).

If cost is an issue, college students are often glad of a chance to snap someone other than their fellow students and family members. Colleges are equipped with excellent photography equipment, and studios, yet the cost is a fraction of what you would pay a commercial photographer.

ADDING A BLOG

You can skip this part of the chapter if you don't have or don't want a blog.

No, don't. Get a blog, they're great.

They are the best way for your readers and potential readers to get to know you. They may not take the risk of buying a book from you if they've never heard of you before – but if they have read your blog and like your writing style, they are more likely to be willing to buy your books, as you won't be completely unknown to them.

They are also excellent for SEO, so if you have a website, having a blog as well will help your website rise up the search engine results pages.

Your followers on Goodreads will be notified when you publish a new blog post, bringing them (hopefully) dashing to your profile to read it and hovering delightfully close to your books!

IMPORT AN EXISTING BLOG

Go to your blog and find your RSS feed. The easiest way is to right-click on a blank part of the screen and select VIEW PAGE SOURCE.

Then search for anything with RSS or FEED. For example, the Goodreads blog has an RSS feed.

COPY that link – which could be similar to either of these types:

www.yourdomain.com/blog_rss

www.yourdomain/sample-feed.xml

Go to your profile by clicking the profile picture thumbnail at the top-right of any Goodreads page. This will take you to your author profile. (If you click the dropdown to the right of your profile picture thumbnail and select EDIT PROFILE, it will take you to your user profile – you can your author profile by selecting EDIT MY AUTHOR PROFILE from that page.)

On the right-hand side, look for a link saying EXTERNAL BLOG FEED URL.

Click CHANGE if the field 'URL' isn't showing.

PASTE in the link you copied earlier then click the checkbox SHOW FULL POST. Click ADD FEED, and you're done.

NOTE: If you started a Goodreads blog and change your mind, you can still connect an external blog to your Goodreads author profile following the steps above.

ADD A NEW GOODREADS BLOG

Log into Goodreads and click VISIT YOUR DASHBOARD on the right-hand side of the page. Click START A BLOG below the 'Your Blog' section:

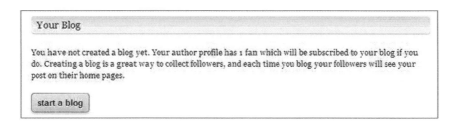

Then click NEW POST and start writing!

The idea of a Goodreads blog is to show your personality and writing, to give readers a feel for

your style. It is very helpful actually, if they enjoy your blog posts they are more likely to buy your books – you aren't an unknown to them.

ADD VIDEO

Video is the latest thing in the world of website promotion. Videos are great for websites as they encourage people to stay on your site longer, to watch the video to the end, thereby improving your bounce rate statistics. They are also more engaging than just words on a screen, they allow people to feel they are getting to know you/your book more.

Video doesn't have to be expensive or complicated. You can make videos yourself using Windows MovieMaker or PowerPoint, or outsource the production on sites such as Fiverr.com, oDesk.com, Freelance.com, or elance.com.

Host it on YouTube for maximum SEO effect (Google own YouTube so give preferential ranking to YouTube content) and paste the YouTube URL into Goodreads so it will show on your profile. You can have more than one video.

It is very easy to add a video, just click ADD NEW next to the Videos section of your profile page.

On YouTube, below your video there should be a SHARE link. Click on that and COPY the URL that appears. Then PASTE that into the Goodreads video box. Enter a title, the code, and a description. Using keywords in your description helps people find your video/book when searching online.

Title*

Video embed html code (from YouTube/Veoh/BookVideos.tv/I

Paste in the code from YouTube.

Video description

Add the description from the YouTube video.

Book this video is about

Select

Channel

trailer

Use the keywords (as tags) that you think your readers will use to find your video/book.

Tags (Comma separated: inspirational, science, humor, etc)

save
cancel

Don't worry too much about what you type in the boxes. The main thing is to paste the code that you copied from YouTube.

FACTS ABOUT VIDEOS

❖ They are free and easy to make using MovieMaker which used to come with Windows computers. It can still be downloaded free from Microsoft.

❖ They can be hosted free on YouTube (and other places) and the URL of the video copied and pasted into Goodreads.

❖ They are good for SEO. When entering the information about the video – on YouTube and on Goodreads – keep SEO in mind. Use the keywords that you think people will use to find your book. This will help your book sales.

❖ They can be put on your website/blog as well.

❖ If you don't feel confident creating your own videos, consider outsourcing the job – it doesn't have to cost a lot.

SPRUCE UP YOUR PROFILE
IF YOU'RE IN A HURRY

- ❖ Use a professional author photo.
- ❖ Import or start a blog.
- ❖ Create or commission a few book trailer-type videos and post them on your profile. Consider adding a video of you or someone else reading a chapter from your latest book. Readers like author interviews – record yourself answering some questions.

Not many authors are making the most of all the features they can add to their profile on Goodreads.

Sophie Kinsella's videos are good, but they are obviously uploaded by her publisher. She doesn't have a blog or anything personal on her profile.

Richelle Mead, on the other hand, is doing it right. She interacts with fans, blogs regularly, posts great videos and gets involved on the site. She doesn't act aloof – she gets as excited about new book releases as her fans do! She is the #4 most followed author on Goodreads.

CHAPTER 6

ALL ABOUT PROFILES

❧❧

GOODREADS PROFILES – USERS AND authors - are public by default and can be viewed by people who aren't Goodreads users. Author profiles are always public, that can't be changed; user profiles can be restricted. When they are public, identifying information isn't viewable and neither are photos, apart from the user profile picture.

If you go to the site without logging in, there will be a section called READERS ONLINE NOW. Click on one of the photos to see that user's public profile. You can usually see some basic information, such as the number of reviews/ratings that person has created, as well as their bookshelves, groups, and updates. You have to sign in to see more information.

Author profiles can be found by either clicking on their books and then clicking the author's name, or by searching for them by name in the Book/ISBN/Author search box on the navigation bar.

As a user you can restrict your profile so that it can only be viewed by other Goodreads (logged-in) users. To do so, go to EDIT PROFILE, then click on the SETTINGS tab.

In the 'Who Can View My Profile' section, you can click to allow anyone (including search engines) to view your profile, or click to prevent that. You can also decide to:

❖ Allow non-friends to follow your reviews.
❖ Allow partners of Goodreads to display your reviews.

- ❖ Allow either a) anyone or b) just your friends to send you private messages.
- ❖ Allow your email address to be shared with a) your friends, or b) no-one.
- ❖ In this section there is also:
- ❖ A challenge question – add a question that only friends would know the answer to, so only genuine friends can send you a friend request.
- ❖ Site customization – choose whether or not to show friend suggestions on your homepage; show friends from Facebook on your homepage; prompt you to recommend books to friends.

Be sure to scroll down to the bottom of the page and click SAVE ACCOUNT SETTINGS to save any changes you have made.

Profiles are similar for both users and authors but there are a few differences:

USER PROFILES

- ❖ A user profile has a little information, followed by favorite books, bookshelves, recent updates, friends in common, friends list and any friends in common, and possibly favorite authors, favorite quotations, currently reading, quizzes.
- ❖ User profiles have their information concentrated on the left-hand side of the page; authors on the right.
- ❖ User profiles look slightly different if you aren't friends with the person – but it isn't like Facebook, where you can't see much at all if you aren't friends. On Goodreads, you can generally see their bookshelves, friends, and recent updates.

AUTHOR PROFILES

- ❖ An author profile usually has – on the right-hand side of the page - a little information, followed by a blog, their books, upcoming events, currently reading, recent updates (includes reviews), topics (in groups) mentioning the author, favorite quotes, groups, favorite authors, and friend comments.
- ❖ On the left-hand side of the page will be video(s), bookshelves, friends in common, friends, and fans.

Goodreads does change things so the layouts mentioned above may change from time-to-time. The quickest way to tell is that the author profile will generally have a BECOME A FAN button (if you aren't already a fan) below their profile picture.

The author page has more options for adding things, so will generally have more on it than a user profile (this is especially true for active Goodreads authors).

Videos and blogs aren't an option for user profiles.

USER/AUTHOR PROFILE FEATURES

YOUR PROFILE INFORMATION

Hover over your profile picture thumbnail on the top right-hand side of any Goodreads page to go to your profile, then click VIEW PROFILE.

You can add/delete information here as well as add/change your profile picture. Some authors use the cover of their latest book as their profile picture.

Consider adding a few lines of biography. It is important to add a little biographical information on your author profile. If you don't, it won't show up around the site.

Also add your website/blog and Twitter handle here, if you have them. This gives readers some background information about you that can help them 'connect' with you - perhaps because you share a love of Sherlock Holmes novels, or you are passionate about deep sea diving or something. It also enables them to find you easily off Goodreads.

We also get the ability to add 'influences' on our profiles (other authors) and our favorite genres. It's a good idea to fill these out - again, it gives readers more chances to feel a connection with you.

Note that authors have two profiles - a user profile and an author profile but they appear as one. Your user profile is the one that makes the profile picture thumbnail at the top right of any Goodreads page. Your author profile is the one that makes the larger profile picture (perhaps of a book cover) that appears on your profile when anyone clicks on it.

YOUR BLOG

You can start a blog right on Goodreads, or import an existing blog, if you have one. If you do that, every time you publish a post on your blog, it will appear on your Goodreads profile. It's a way of populating your Goodreads presence without actually spending time on Goodreads!

YOUR BOOKS

Your own books will appear here - the ones you have published.

YOUR EVENTS

You can add events here such as book signings, launch dates, any speaking engagements or conferences you are scheduled to attend.

RECENT UPDATES

This will show your Goodreads activity, such as books you have shelved, updates/blog posts you have liked, groups you have joined, authors you are following.

QUOTATIONS

You can add your own quotations here or those of others (e.g. famous quotes). It's a good idea to add lines from your own books here.

You aren't restricted to this section for adding quotes, though. If other authors have posted their favorite quotations on their profiles, you can click the LIKE button so you can add your favorites to your own profile – just one click does it.

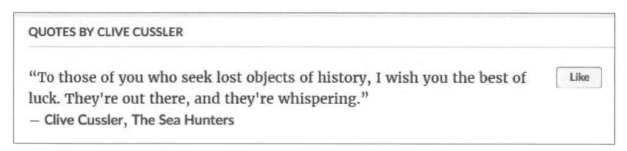

> QUOTES BY CLIVE CUSSLER
>
> "To those of you who seek lost objects of history, I wish you the best of luck. They're out there, and they're whispering."
> — Clive Cussler, The Sea Hunters
>
> Like

Go to your profile and the new quotation will have magically appeared. Other people can Like the original quote on your profile.

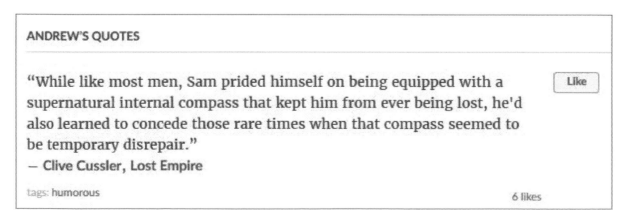

> ANDREW'S QUOTES
>
> "While like most men, Sam prided himself on being equipped with a supernatural internal compass that kept him from ever being lost, he'd also learned to concede those rare times when that compass seemed to be temporary disrepair."
> — Clive Cussler, Lost Empire
>
> Like
>
> tags: humorous   6 likes

You can change the order of quotations by clicking EDIT next to the QUOTES [YOU] LIKES. This will take you to a screen with up and down arrows to adjust the order. Click SAVE POSITION CHANGES when done.

GROUPS

Groups you have joined will be listed here. If you join groups relevant to the genre(s) you write in you could make connections with readers who read in that genre.

FAVORITE AUTHORS

These appear on your profile if you have clicked the ADD TO MY FAVORITE AUTHORS link below the profile picture of any Goodreads author. Choose authors in your genre (you want your books ranked alongside theirs, you want to be associated with them), as well as some big names.

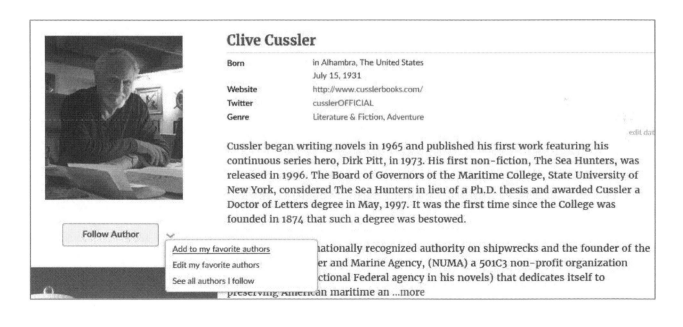

PROFILES IF YOU'RE IN A HURRY

➢ Author profiles are recognizable by the presence of a blog, videos, etc.

➢ Add favorite quotations to your profile by clicking LIKE on the quotations on other people's profiles.

➢ Add quotations from your own books (you could also turn these into tweets for extra marketing value!).

➢ Join relevant groups to make connections with potential readers.

➢ Become fans of other authors and add some favorite authors so they will appear on your profile and be associated with you. Choose some in your own genre(s) to be strategic.

CHAPTER 7

ALL ABOUT BOOKSHELVES

GOODREADS REVOLVES AROUND BOOKSHELVES. They are the nuts and bolts of the whole site. Your own and other people's bookshelves are of vital importance but many people find them daunting and don't know how to use them.

They were the thing that I found most daunting when I joined Goodreads, as I didn't understand them. Then I realized there is nothing to understand! They're just there, virtual shelves that you plonk books on just like you would at home.

I don't understand my numerous physical bookshelves at home, I just use them. That's what you need to do with your Goodreads bookshelves.

Click on MY BOOKS, which will be at the top of the screen when you log into Goodreads, to see your own bookshelves. Go to any friend or other Goodreads user (including authors) to see their bookshelves.

When people add your book to their shelves, or review it, you will be able to tell by going to your book and clicking REVIEWS or RATINGS.

There will be a list of reviews, ratings, and people who have added it to shelves. You have an opportunity to click a button to 'Like' reviews.

Goodreads doesn't recommend that authors do anything to thank people who have added their books to their own shelves. They warn that it could be considered spammy.

Fair point, because if a lot of people added your book to their shelves and you thanked all of them, your news stream would be full of your own comments, all the same, or very similar. It would look a bit suspicious.

HOW TO ADD A BOOK TO YOUR SHELVES

Type in a book's name in the search box. Click on the book so see its page. Then either click the green 'Want To Read' button to add the book to your 'To Read' shelf or hover over the little green button showing three books and a new menu will appear.

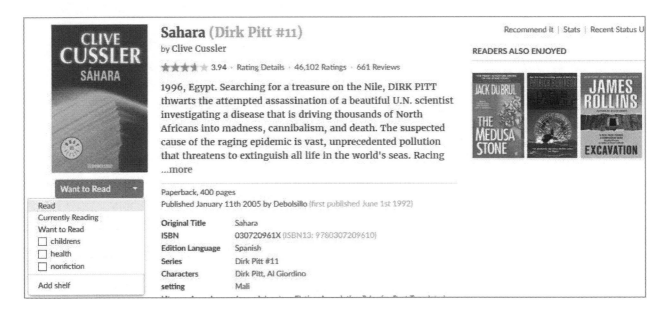

This lets you choose one of your shelves (or more than one if you wish) to put the book on. If you are new to Goodreads you may just have the three that come with a user account (Read, Currently Reading, Want To Read).

You can click ADD SHELF to add a new shelf.

Notice that it also shows other books that are similar to the one you are shelving. I find this really helpful when I have read all the books my favorite authors have produced!

There is the option – if you have connected your Facebook account to your Goodreads account – to post the news on Facebook that you have just added a book to one of your shelves.

I don't recommend this if you are adding a lot of books to your shelves. It's spammy. Your Facebook friends are going to get pretty fed up of hearing about your reading preferences if a stream of messages about books you have liked appears on their walls. Just click the checkbox to deselect this option. You can reselect it at a later date if you are just adding one book at a time.

I often choose to publish my reviews on Facebook but that is because they are less frequent. I put books on my shelves all the time!

If you add a book to your 'Read' shelf, you will be asked to rate and/or review it.

Rating takes just a click, choose one of the stars.

Reviewing takes longer but is a good idea. You only need to write a sentence or two. Reviewing seems to tell the Goodreads algorithm that you are a committed Goodreads user. It makes you more likely to win when entering Giveaways as well (see the Giveaways section).

At the bottom of the review window, there are checkboxes. You can choose whether or not to post the review to your Goodreads blog, and to add it to

your Goodreads update feed. Update feed is, by default, preselected so you will need to click on that box to deselect it if you don't want your review to appear in the newsfeeds of your Goodreads friends.

Note that when you search for a book, Goodreads will show you if there are any groups with that book mentioned in them. This is of particular interest to us as authors – we want our books mentioned in groups.

You can find books by searching, in groups, in ads around the site, and various other ways. Click on a book's cover image or name to see more information about it, and to add it to your shelves.

At the top right-hand corner of a book's page there will be links:

Recommend it | Stats | Recent status updates
READERS ALSO ENJOYED

You can recommend it to friends, view statistics (a graph of when it was added to shelves on Goodreads), or see if it has been featured in any recent status updates. This will show the profile pictures of people who are reading it, their progress and comments about it. The 'Readers Also Enjoyed' links are to books that Goodreads consider similar to the one being looked at. They are generally books from traditional publishers and not always very similar!

'MY BOOKS' PAGE

Click MY BOOKS from the top navigation bar on any Goodreads page to be taken to your bookshelves.

Here you can see at a glance the number of books you have in total, as well as on each shelf. You can view the books by their covers, or in table format, with different columns of information showing. You can choose to show or hide columns such as author name, date published, date purchased, etc.

If you click EDIT next to any of your books, you can go into them to change/add a rating and/or review, or to change the shelf you keep it on. I like to keep my Read books on more than one shelf – the Read shelf itself, as well as a genre shelf for the book.

TOOLS ON THE 'MY BOOKS' PAGE

ADD SHELF

New shelves can be added when you add books to your shelves, but they can also be added here. You can have as many shelves as you want.

Be sure to have at least one shelf for every genre you write in. You can often split your genres - so you could have a Children's shelf, a Children's Fiction shelf, a Picture Books shelf, etc.

ADD FAVORITE SHELF

On the My Books page, click EDIT SHELVES. You can choose to feature one shelf at the top of your profile.

My Profile > My Books > Edit Shelves					
shelf	feature	sortable	sticky	exclusive	recs
read (112)	○	☐	☐	☑	☐
currently-reading (4)	○	☑	☐	☑	☐
to-read (137)	○	☑	☐	☑	☑
x childrens-fiction (11) rename	●	☑	☑	☐	☑
x gardening-selfsufficiency (10) rename	○	☐	☐	☐	☑
x health (7) rename	○	☐	☐	☐	☑
x influences (1) rename	○	☑	☐	☐	☑
x teens (2) rename	○	☐	☐	☐	☑
x veggie (7) rename	○	☐	☐	☐	☑

Clicking the 'Sortable' checkboxes will enable you to customize the order of your shelves.

Clicking the 'Sticky' checkboxes will make the books sort first. I have the genre that my latest book is in marked as Sticky.

Clicking 'Exclusive' means that a book can only appear on one of these shelves (i.e. you can't have a book on 'Read' at the same time as it is on 'Currently Reading').

Clicking 'Recs' will prompt the Goodreads Recommendations Engine to try to make recommendations for books on that shelf – this is VERY important to do for shelves in any way connected to any genres you write in.

OWNED BOOKS

When you add a book to your shelves you have the opportunity to tick a box to say that you own it. This is to allow you to keep track of your books – handy if you are in the habit of lending them out and forgetting who you have loaned them to.

You could also have a LOANED shelf. If you're going to be that organized, add a BORROWED shelf as well so you remember to give books back!

RECOMMENDATIONS

This takes you to the Recommendations page, which will be individual to your reading habits. It will have book suggestions based on your shelves.

These tend to be the very popular books, so this isn't as useful for people like me who enjoy reading undiscovered authors.

WIDGETS

Widgets are great for showing your presence on Goodreads elsewhere – such as on a website or blog. You can customize each widget and grab the code, ready to put on your site or send to your designer.

Showing your bookshelves on your site is a good way of connecting to people. They will feel they know you more and perhaps have things in common with you.

IMPORT/EXPORT

If you have had a lifetime of prolific reading, it is going to take a while to add everything you have ever read to Goodreads. Now that Amazon owns Goodreads, we can easily import our Amazon purchases and add them to our Goodreads bookshelves.

Go to the MY BOOKS page and there should be a notice at the top of the window asking if you would like to import your Amazon book purchases:

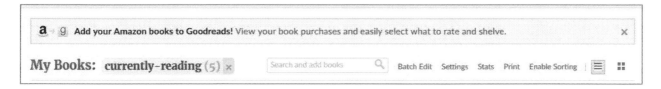

You don't have to add everything you've bought on Amazon to your shelves. You're given an opportunity to choose which books you want to add.

If you already have your books listed somewhere else – perhaps in a spreadsheet – you can import them straight into Goodreads. On the MY BOOKS page there is an IMPORT link on the left-hand side.

I'm not that organized! My daughter is, though. She has all her books listed, so she can easily see which ones are missing from her physical shelves at home. Goodreads is wonderful for her as she has imported her entire collection of books (hundreds!) and, when shopping in bookstores, can access Goodreads on her smartphone to see what she has/doesn't have (she is passionate about keeping bookstores open, so tries to shop in physical shops as much as possible. My credit card does not agree with her!).

You can also import books from web pages, as long as they have an ISBN. All you have to do is export from the other site (e.g. Shelfari) to a .xls, .csv[2], or .txt file. Then import the file to Goodreads. Bear in mind that not all books will be on Goodreads so you may have a few that it doesn't recognize.

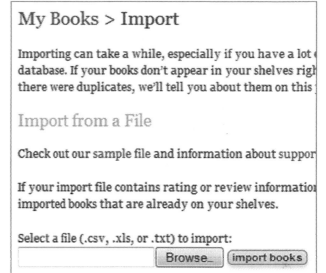

If you haven't used Shelfari before it is quite simple. You can register and then log in with your Amazon account. When logged in, go to your Account Settings and click the SHELF tab, then DOWNLOAD A LIST OF YOUR BOOKS.

Save the file, then go back to MY BOOKS in Goodreads. Click IMPORT/EXPORT. Click BROWSE to find your downloaded file (see right):

Then click IMPORT BOOKS. This can take a while. Goodreads gives you a link to see your import.

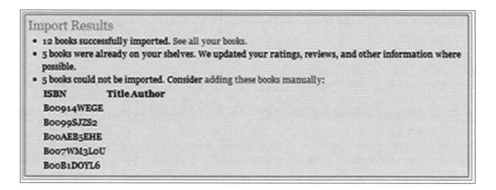

You have the option to manually add any books that didn't import. This is how the Goodreads database grows, by all of us adding books they don't know about.

FIND DUPLICATES

This is for finding duplicates of editions of books. Duplicates take into account different editions of books - you may actually have two different editions though.

---

[2] Goodreads say that csv imports work best.

SHELF CLOUD

This is a jazzy visual representation – an infographic – of your shelves, showing which have the most books on them. You can sort it either by shelf size or shelf name.

MOST READ AUTHORS

This shows you which authors you have read the most. Mine are Mary Higgins Clark, followed by Stephanie Meyer, Malcolm Gladwell, Oscar Wilde, and Dick Strawbridge (a self-sufficiency hero in the UK).

STATS

This shows you graphs showing how many books you read/rated by year.

API

API stands for Application Programming Interface. This is for really serious Star Trek Convention-type techies. I can say that because it includes me! It is the code that developers need when writing software that they want to 'talk' to Goodreads.

BOOKSHELVES
IF YOU'RE IN A HURRY

❖ Bookshelves are great, don't be daunted by them. You'll soon get the hang of adding books to your To Read shelf by hovering over the green buttons on book pages. You can hover again to add them to additional shelves.

❖ When you rate or review books they are automatically added to your Read shelf. You can add them to another shelf as well, but not instead of the Read shelf, only in addition to.

❖ Make books on the shelves in your chosen genre appear first by marking them as Sticky.

❖ Make sure you choose RECS on the Edit Shelves page for shelves related to genres that you write in – that way the Goodreads Recommendations Engine will try to recommend books in your genre (s).

❖ Make new shelves and edit your shelves from your MY BOOKS page.

CHAPTER 8

MAKING FRIENDS
& INFLUENCING READERS

THE HOKEY-POKEY IS not what it is all about – this is! Goodreads is about books and readers – not authors and their pressing need to sell books. Making friends is the first and most important thing you need to do on Goodreads. Make friends, interact, talk about books – that's what it's all about.

You can be friends with other Goodreads users. You can be fans of Goodreads authors. You can also be both – as long as each user hasn't reached the 5,000 friend maximum limit.

Every author is also (or should be!) a reader, which is why they have a combined user and author profile. Their profile lists their reading habits, links to their own books, and as authors they can add additional gizmos.

People will approach you, often because they feel they have something in common with you – shared books – or because you have chatted in a group discussion.

When someone sends you a friend request, there will be a red notification to the right of the little envelope icon, next to your profile picture thumbnail.

Click on the friends icon and you will have the option to either approve or ignore the request.

HOW TO FIND GOODREADS FRIENDS

Rather than wait for people to approach you, there are a number of ways to proactively find friends.

IMPORT CONTACTS

Click on the Friends icon at the top of the screen, just to the left of your profile thumbnail picture.

Then click ADD FRIENDS on the right of the page.

There are currently five options for importing contacts from elsewhere on the Internet:

- ❖ Facebook
- ❖ Gmail
- ❖ Yahoo Mail
- ❖ Hotmail
- ❖ Twitter

Click on any of these to find the people you know from that platform who are also on Goodreads. You can then click the checkboxes next to those names and click ADD FRIENDS.

FACEBOOK

The Facebook link puts friends in categories according to your reading tastes.

You can either click ADD to add them all, or click on the genre name to see the individuals - then select or deselect them as you wish before clicking ADD at the bottom of the window.

GMAIL

Goodreads asks for access to your Google Contacts. Click GRANT ACCESS to continue.

You should then see a list of people who are on Goodreads who are also in your Google Contacts. You can choose to UNCHECK ALL or CHECK ALL.

I always uncheck all and go through carefully. Sometimes there are people you don't want to get too personal with - for example if you have been emailing your bank manager!

There may also be a 'Friends of Friends' section. I never bother with this.

YAHOO MAIL

Works in a similar way to Gmail.

HOTMAIL

The Hotmail connection sometimes takes a few attempts – it doesn't seem to trust Goodreads.

When you eventually break through, you are greeted with a similar screen to the one for Gmail, with a list of contacts and the ability to select or deselect them before clicking ADD FRIENDS.

TWITTER

Again, you have the option to select or deselect as you prefer and connect to any of your Twitter contacts who are on Goodreads.

At the bottom of the page there is an option to click a checkbox to send a tweet to share Goodreads with Twitter followers.

When anyone sends me a friend request I tend to check out their profile before approving it. Often they are authors and, if they have a book that interests me, I will add it to my To Read shelf.

Obviously, as authors, there is a big temptation there. There is a chance that people we approach will add our books to their shelves. So there is a temptation to approach lots and lots of people! Not a good idea.

It is absolutely fine if it is someone you have chatted to in a group, or perhaps you have a friend in common, have compared books, and realize you enjoy similar books. That's OK – as a one-off.

If you do it more than once, and/or on a regular basis, it not only looks a bit fishy but it could bring you to the attention of Goodreads librarians or staff. They take a dim view of spammy, self-promoting behavior, because it brings the whole tone of the site down.

USE GOODREADS WIDGETS

Goodreads provides various widgets for authors to add to their websites or blogs.

These announce their presence on Goodreads and give their website visitors a chance to hop over to Goodreads to check out their books.

More on widgets in Section Three.

ANNOUNCE YOUR PRESENCE ON GOODREADS USING EXISTING CHANNELS

Don't underestimate the power of existing contacts – on and offline. A number of highly successful authors I know are in the habit of carrying business cards showing numerous ways of contacting them, including their Goodreads profile URL.

If you go to, or have ever been to, offline networking meetings, you probably have dozens of business cards littering a drawer. Dig them out and renew contact! A simple 'How are you doing' email with a link to your Goodreads profile in your signature can reap rewards – and enquiries. Here is an excellent article on making the most of your email signature:

http://buildbookbuzz.com/turn-your-e-mail-signature-into-a-book-marketing-machine

Announce your Goodreads membership on your blog, social media accounts (don't forget LinkedIn – if you don't have a presence on there it is a good idea to establish one, as mentioned earlier, LinkedIn is marvelous for SEO). There are some excellent groups for authors on LinkedIn. I'm in a number and find them helpful and encouraging.

SORT YOUR FRIENDS

To get to a list of your friends, click on the little icon of two people which is just to the left of your profile thumbnail picture at the top-right of the Goodreads screen – that's the Friends link.

The list on this page can be sorted in a number of ways, by:

- ❖ First name.
- ❖ Last name.
- ❖ Last online.
- ❖ Last status.
- ❖ Date added.
- ❖ Books added.
- ❖ Number of friends.
- ❖ Top friends.
- ❖ Last review.

I use all of these at different times. It is a fabulous feature – much more useful than Facebook's sorting order, which is either Top stories (where Facebook choose which status updates they think are most important to you – i.e. which are paying them the most), or Recent.

Being able to sort by reviews, last status, last online, etc., is very handy.

Notice that the Currently Reading book choice of your friends will be showing. The book you are currently reading can be seen by anyone on Goodreads. Make it a good one!

ADD TOP FRIENDS

You may want to add some people as top friends, so you will be able to find them easily.

Click EDIT FRIENDS, to the right of the alphabet above the list of friends. This will bring up the option of clicking beside each friend's name to make them a Top Friend. Click DONE EDITING when done.

The people I add as my top friends tend to be:

- ❖ Family
- ❖ Friends
- ❖ People I chat to regularly on Goodreads and elsewhere
- ❖ Authors who are in my Goodreads, Facebook or LinkedIn groups
- ❖ People I admire, I follow them to learn from how they do things!

While you are looking at your list of friends, you may notice that some of them are online – there will be a red ONLINE notice under their names. There isn't a way of chatting real-time like there is on Facebook but you can send a message (see below) and, as they are on the site, they will receive a notification straightaway and may reply.

ADD A STORY

For each friend, you can add some information about your connection, or a few words about how you met.

Be aware that this will be displayed on your Goodreads profile – but only after they have verified the story.

You do have to click in at least one of the checkboxes but you don't have to add anything in the 'Story – how do you and XYZ know each other?' box.

When you have added a story the 'Add A Story' link will have disappeared from their name on your friends list and been replaced by 'View Friend Details'.

I don't use this facility very much but there may be times when it could be useful. Perhaps you met someone at a conference – the reminder of that two years later, when you have probably forgotten, would be handy!

MESSAGES

The Goodreads internal messaging system is a little like an email program, with a list of messages showing who they are from, the subject, and the date.

To find your messages, click on the little envelope which sits between the 'g' notifications icon and the Friends icon, at the top-right of the navigation bar.

There is an Inbox, a Saved box, a Sent box, and a Trash box. You can read, reply, and delete messages.

To send a message, though, you need to go to a friend's profile and click Send A Message, which is beneath their profile picture, next to Compare Books.

You can generally send messages to non-friends too.

Note that not all authors are on Goodreads, even though their books may be, so obviously you won't be able to message them if they don't have a Goodreads profile.

SEND A MESSAGE

Click on the person's name in your friend list and, on their profile page, click SEND MESSAGE.

Cathy (cathy.presland@b...com) is your friend
send message | recommend book | compare books | write a story | suggest friends

A new page 'Compose New Message' will appear with subject and message boxes.

Enter your message and click SEND or PREVIEW.

The friend will receive a notification next to the friend icon, at the right-hand side of the top navigation bar.

It is a good idea to send a message to thank people for connecting on Goodreads - not with a list of your books and a request for reviews, just a no-strings thanks.

COMPARE BOOKS

Go to anyone's Goodreads profile – friend or stranger – and you will probably have the ability to Compare Books. There will be a link under their name on their profile page, alongside the Send Message | Recommend Book links.

This takes you to a page where you can see which books you have in common on your Read shelves and how their rating compared to yours, as well as statistics about how their reading habits compare to yours.

I have found friends through this. There's nothing like having favorite books in common to start a friendship.

Apart from the books you have in common on your Read shelf, you can also go through the other books they have read to see if you have actually read them but not got around to adding them to your shelves yet. This is really handy.

Another thing the Compare Books facility offers you is a similarity section. Here's mine with my friend Karen.

I haven't seen Karen for years – we used to go to the same church about a decade ago – and I was pleased when she popped up as a Goodreads user when I did a Facebook import of my contacts. We both love Mary Higgins Clark and Rebecca Shaw books, and have similar feelings about other genres and authors. It's lovely to be back in touch and have things to talk about.

Here is a comparison of my reading habits with those of Otis Chandler, one of the founders of Goodreads:

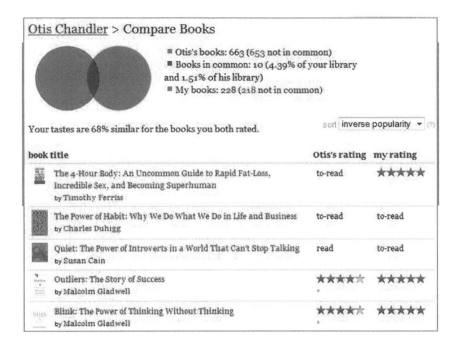

I don't think we have enough in common to forge a friendship just yet!

MAKING FRIENDS
IF YOU'RE IN A HURRY

- ❖ Import contacts from other sites - Facebook, Twitter, email accounts.
- ❖ Add Goodreads widgets to your website/blog.
- ❖ Add your Goodreads profile URL to your email signature, business cards, and marketing literature.
- ❖ If you are in any author groups on or offline, ask if anyone wants to connect on Goodreads.
- ❖ Get chatting in group discussions, get to know people.

CHAPTER 9

ALL ABOUT GROUPS

❧

WHAT OTHER SITES CALL Forums, Goodreads calls Groups. Well it is good to be a bit different!

From the early days of just being a nice place for virtual discussions, Groups have become one of the most powerful tools on the site. Even Oprah has joined! There is an official Oprah Book Club on Goodreads, free for anyone to join.

Groups are like mini sites. They contain a forum and can also have:

- ❖ Group Home.
- ❖ Events – virtual and physical events can be listed.
- ❖ Invite People – invite friends to join the group if you think it is something that will interest them. Don't spam them though.
- ❖ Bookshelf – books that users have chosen for the group's bookshelf (not the same as personal bookshelves). Some groups only allow moderators to add books to the group bookshelf, others will allow users. If they do, there will be an ADD BOOKS link on the bookshelf, which you can click on to add relevant books.
- ❖ Photos – generally these are past profile pictures of the group. Sometimes groups have the a picture of the book the group is currently reading as their profile picture.
- ❖ Members – a list of the members and moderators of the group. Generally you will see any Goodreads friends of yours who are members of the group in a separate section, then the rest of the members underneath that. You can sort

members by: Last online; Number of comments (made in that group); Date joined: Number of books (on Goodreads shelves); First name.

❖ Discussions – the place to hang out and meet people.

❖ Videos – moderators can upload videos, some groups allow members to upload as well.

Some groups exist to connect authors and readers. Within those there will be some eye-watering chances to plug your book. See the screenshot below from the Making Connections group, asking authors to post if they are seeking reviews. Open goal!

Discussion > ARR: Authors Requesting Reviews

new topic

topics (showing 1-4 of 4)	started by	posts	views	last activity▲
* Authors Sign Up	Tana , *The Wise*	1433 (1433 new)	1425	2 hours, 58 min ago
Latest ARR Books	Midu , *The Magnificent*	23 (23 new)	268	Feb 06, 2013 05:42am
Changes to the ARR Program - Effective July 2012	Sheri , *The Just*	1 (1 new)	298	Jul 01, 2012 12:52am
How the ARR Program Works	Sheri , *The Just*	3 (3 new)	421	Jun 29, 2012 04:08am

Go to **www.goodreads.com/group**. Not group**s**, group. Goodreads really does like to be different! There will be lists of different groups, usually:

❖ Featured Groups.

❖ Recently Active Groups.

❖ New Groups.

❖ Groups In Your Country.

❖ Official Groups.

❖ Author Groups.

Once you have joined some, there will also be MY GROUPS towards the top of the Group page. On the right-hand side of the page will be the BROWSE BY TAG section, where you can click on the various genres of groups. You can also search for a group using the FIND GROUPS feature at the top of the page.

You can then sort the groups by:

- ❖ Popular (number of members)
- ❖ Recently Popular (most new members in the last few days)
- ❖ Recently Active (groups that people have most recently posted in)
- ❖ Near Me (geographically close to you – handy for posting about physical events such as book signings and tours)
- ❖ New (recently-created groups)
- ❖ My Books (once you have joined some)

The Popular and Recently Active groups are a good indication of the liveliness of the group. Size of the group isn't as important as how active it is. Small groups can be very active and the members get to know each other more than they do in the very large groups.

It is good to join a few different types of groups – large, small, and genre-specific. Be sure to join groups in genres that you love to read in, then you will be able to contribute to the discussion!

HOW TO JOIN A GROUP

Click on the group's name then click JOIN GROUP.

It isn't like Facebook where you generally have to wait for an Admin to approve your request to join. I haven't come across a Goodreads group that doesn't allow immediate access (but there may be some).

SOME POPULAR/ACTIVE GROUPS

It's a good idea to keep an eye on the largest groups as it gives you a feel for the latest trends in the book world and what is capturing people's attention. Paranormal romance (Twilight-type) is still riding high.

Some of the largest groups on Goodreads are:

- ❖ Paranormal Romance & Urban Fantasy
- ❖ The Sword & Laser
- ❖ Boxall's 1001 Books You Must Read Before You Die
- ❖ The Next Best Book Club
- ❖ ! POETRY!

I would advise joining a large group, perhaps one in your own genre or maybe in a genre you would like to write in. Joining a large group puts you in touch with thousands of Goodreads readers. Make connections, join in discussions. Don't try to sell your books.

This one is one of the better-known Goodreads groups:

THE NEXT BEST BOOK CLUB

www.goodreads.com/group/join/1218-the-next-best-book-club

It has a massive membership and is very active. It has been featured in the New York Times.

Eventually, the ideal is for groups you are in to feature one of your books and chat about it with you. However there is one group in particular that you don't, as an author, ever want to be mentioned in. It is ...

BADLY BEHAVING AUTHORS

www.goodreads.com/group/show/68876-badly-behaving-authors

This was founded by people who were fed up with authors who attacked them for writing negative reviews of their books.

The general rule for authors on Goodreads is not to respond to negative reviews but some people just can't help themselves and get into unfortunate slanging matches with people who have reviewed their books as anything other than wonderful. This group names and shames those authors.

(If you have ever struggled with the emotional impact of a negative review, you might want to check out Tom Oberbichler's book, *Bad Reviews - How to make good use of Feedback*. It can really help.)

GOODREADS LIBRARIANS GROUP

www.goodreads.com/group/show/220-goodreads-librarians-group

The most popular group on Goodreads is the Librarians Group. It is possible to become a librarian yourself, when you have rated 50+ books.

This is one group that you will probably have to visit. When you list your own book on Goodreads it is fairly quick and easy to get it listed – but generally it will appear without its cover. Goodreads advises authors to post a note in the Librarians Group asking for someone to upload their cover. So this is a group to join!

It isn't just for adding covers. It is also possible to ask for someone to combine your book editions, add chapter metadata, delete books, deal with book series, and make other suggestions for books and the book catalogue.

You post a request and a Goodreads Librarian will respond and correct the problem for you. I have found that they are very quick and efficient at doing so.

Librarians can edit book and author data, add book covers, and combine different editions of books. They correct problems in the Goodreads catalogue, basically.

Find the Librarian Manual at:

www.goodreads.com/librarian_manual

You can apply to become a librarian if you have 50+ books on your shelves (that you have read – not written!). Go to www.goodreads.com/about/apply_librarian.

As the Librarians group is so large, it is a good idea to turn off email notifications once you have had any request actioned, or you will get fed up with the bombardment of notifications (see Group Notifications, below).

OPRAH'S BOOK CLUB 2.0 (OFFICIAL)

www.goodreads.com/group/show/85538-oprah-s-book-club-2-0-official

This really is approved by Oprah herself – it frequently contains her personal notes, and her favorite quotes from the currently-read book. Like a book club in the physical world, Oprah's Goodreads book club choose a new book every month, all read it, and then discuss it. They choose a wide range of books from novels to biographies/autobiographies to nonfiction.

Oprah has a huge following and getting to know her followers could give you a better understanding of upcoming trends.

GOODREADS AUTHORS/READERS

www.goodreads.com/group/show/26989-goodreads-authors-readers

Currently 9,054 members. It is split into genres, which is handy – you can find the section you need easily – and has very lively discussions.

GROUPS TO GET YOUR BOOK NOTICED

MAKING CONNECTIONS

www.goodreads.com/group/show/60696-making-connections

This group has hundreds of books listed to read and review. The group exists to connect authors with readers, bloggers, publishers and reviewers. They help authors promote their books (you can ask for help) with blog tours, interviews, reviews, etc.

When you join the group you can go to DISCUSSIONS on the right-hand side of the page and find the ARR (Authors Requesting Reviews) thread. Click the AUTHORS SIGN UP link and add the details of your book. They will do the rest.

Be careful to only promote your books in threads like this. No-one will put up with spammers.

You can also search for other groups which focus on authors by …

SEARCHING FOR GROUPS

If you do a search for the Making Connections group, you will see similar groups come up as suggestions. The Goodreads algorithm pulls in groups with similar keywords and content. This is very handy. Searching for the keywords of your book or genre is a great idea. So if you have written a book about the Tudor period, it would be a good idea to join groups with 'Tudor' in their keywords.

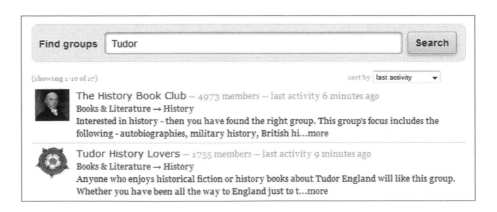

GROUP NOTIFICATIONS

There are times when you want to receive all notifications from a group – particularly when they involve things you are passionate about – but they can also get annoying.

Turn them on/off by clicking on your profile picture thumbnail at the top right of the Goodreads screen, then selecting EDIT PROFILE.

Next, scroll down to GROUP EMAIL PREFERENCES and select your notification preferences. You can choose to receive notifications as individual emails, email digests, Goodreads site notification only, both site notification & email, or no notifications at all.

There are checkboxes at the bottom of the screen where you can change the default notification settings for when you comment on groups, follow discussions, or when one of your groups is about to start reading a book. The options are for daily or weekly notification alerts.

I have actually turned all email notifications off because I'm on Goodreads so much that I prefer to read them on the site itself. Notifications appear to the left of your profile picture thumbnail at the top-right of the Goodreads screen. It's the little 'g' icon.

If you prefer email notifications, add 'no-reply@mail.goodreads.com' to your email contacts list. This should ensure you receive all emails from Goodreads.

HOW TO CREATE A GROUP

It isn't difficult, just click the CREATE A GROUP link on the Groups page. Goodreads recommends creating your own group, as an author, once you have either:

❖ 100 friends or more - any less than that and you wouldn't have enough initial interest in order to make the group look busy and interesting enough for others to want to join
❖ More than 500 reviews

It isn't difficult to start a group (see instructions below) and you don't need anything to start one.

It is a good idea to create a masthead image. If you are particularly gifted graphically, by all means do it yourself. Canva.com is a good site to use for simple social media graphics. If not, it is worth outsourcing it. You can get a decent image created on Fiverr.com from $5.

HOW TO ADD AN EVENT TO A GROUP

At the top of the Goodreads screen, COMMUNITY > EVENTS then click ADD AN EVENT (right-hand side).

Add the details, including start and end dates. You could call it an 'Ask The Author', 'Book Discussion', or whatever you want.

Goodreads suggests:

❖ Aiming to attract at least 20 people as that is the minimum needed for a lively discussion.

❖ Host a discussion on a single day.

❖ Starting a single discussion topic – and all questions will go in that thread, which makes them easier to find and respond to.

You can then add a video or some information to hook people into joining in.

Have a look through the popular and active groups to see what they are doing and find ways of doing similar things in your own group.

While on the Events page, you can search for events local to you – or local to where you will be if you are going on a trip. It's good to meet people in the real world, and you can take along some business cards with details of your books on them!

FEATURED AUTHOR GROUPS

A Featured Author Group is a discussion group about and for an author or authors. It is possible to create a group yourself and just for a single day.

Once you have a good number of books published with multiple reviews on each, and a strong fan base, you could start a group.

Readers love to chat with authors. Goodreads suggests waiting, though, until you have enough people who would be likely to join, otherwise you run the risk of running a bit of a lonely party.

Goodreads recommends:

- ❖ Adding videos. Videos are good to sit back and watch. Not everyone wants to get into lengthy discussions.
- ❖ Keeping it simple. They suggest a one-day group.
- ❖ Promoting it. Blog, tweet, and Facebook about it.

Go to: **www.goodreads.com/group/new** to create a new group. It really is best to wait until you have a following though.

GETTING REVIEWS FROM GROUP MEMBERS

A number of groups – such as the 'Making Connections' one (they have a YA one as well) – have threads where authors can request reviews. The ones I have used have a space where authors can write a little about their book and the formats it is available in. Then Goodreads users who are interested can respond and ask for a copy in the format of their choosing.

Just a day after I posted my first message requesting reviews I received a Goodreads message from one of the moderators of the Making Connections group with two review requests.

So all I had to do was send two copies of my book in EPUB format to the email addresses given. It's a great arrangement and totally fine with Amazon. These aren't paid reviewers, these were Goodreads users who were interested in my book and its genre. Wonderful.

GROUPS
IF YOU'RE IN A HURRY

A tip I used to give when I taught social media involved groups on LinkedIn, and it works on Goodreads, although slightly differently. On LinkedIn you aren't allowed to send connection requests to people outside your immediate circle of contacts – friends of friends (second degree contacts) are OK but people who don't have any connections similar to you are beyond your reach (these are third degree contacts).

However, if you are in the same *group* as the person you want to connect with, you can send them a friend request - even if you don't know any of their contacts.

As an author, you want to be doing something similar on Goodreads, namely:

- ❖ Follow a few groups in your genre (s). Be sure to follow the group rules.
- ❖ Chat to people in discussion threads.
- ❖ Only then should you add people as friends – make it people you have communicated with several times in groups, people who have similar book preferences to you (use the Compare Books feature by going to any member's profile and clicking COMPARE BOOKS. If you have lots in common that's a good excuse to connect!).

In groups you can also:

- ❖ Connect with authors who are really getting it right
- ❖ Connect with your existing readers
- ❖ Connect with your potential readers
- ❖ Befriend the moderator(s)
- ❖ Consider doing an author chat, they are popular. Make sure you have lots of reviews and a good number of your books on people's shelves. That gives you an indication that your chat will be reasonably popular.

A lot of people are very enthusiastic about the benefits of Goodreads groups, not least bloggers. Check out this post from Lori Hettler of The Next Best Book Club:

www.girl-who-reads.com/2012/05/tips-on-thursday-goodreads-groups.html

Groups are listed on people's profiles (towards the bottom of the page). If there is someone you want to connect with, join one of the groups that they are in. Then you will be able to interact with them in discussions.

You will be putting your profile within their reach. It also makes you look more 'connected' to others – hob-knobbing with well-known authors seems to put you in their category of success!

CHAPTER 10

RECOMMENDATIONS

There are a number of ways to recommend books to others and have them recommended to you. The Recommendations Engine part of Goodreads is another powerful opportunity for authors.

Goodreads helpfully offers recommendations to you based on your existing book choices – the books on your shelves. They only start to make recommendations when you have rated a minimum of 20 books on your shelves – without them their algorithm doesn't have enough to work with.

The more books you rate, the more Goodreads learns what to recommend for you in future.

The Recommendations page is at:

http://www.goodreads.com/recommendations

Or you can click on BROWSE > RECOMMENDATIONS.

Yours will be populated (assuming you have 20 or more books on your own shelves that you have **rated**) with books in categories, based on the types of books you enjoy. You will also have sections based specifically on your Read and To Read shelves. There will be a few books in each section and you can usually click MORE FOR THIS GENRE to see more recommendations.

You can start to teach Goodreads what to recommend you by clicking either WANT TO READ or NOT INTERESTED on each book. Books that you want to read will get a green tick under them. Books that you are not interested in will appear slightly grayed out. This works well – Goodreads just gets better and better at finding books that you will like.

You can display the book recommendations either as book covers or as a list.

If you hover over a book you will see a popup with a short description and why that book was recommended to you, which is a thumbnail of its cover after the words, 'Because you added …'

HOW TO RECOMMEND A BOOK TO A FRIEND

Go to the book's page and click RECOMMEND IT on the top right-hand side of the screen. (If you try to recommend one of your own books, Goodreads will give an error message that you can't recommend your own books.) Type the friend's name in the box that appears:

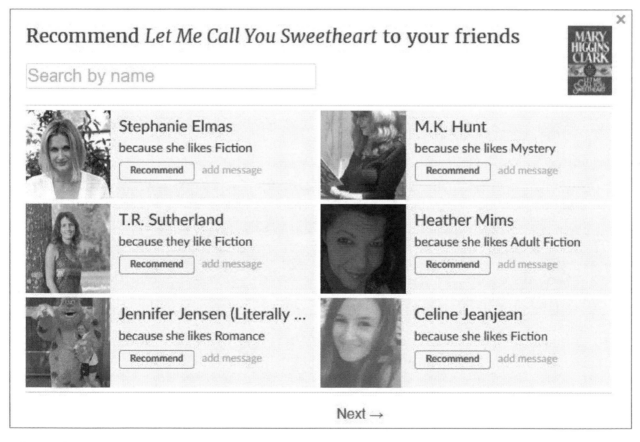

They will receive an inoffensive email inviting them to 'check it out'.

RECOMMENDATIONS
IF YOU'RE IN A HURRY

❖ What you need to do is *get users on Goodreads to add your book(s) and others in the same genre* to one of their shelves. That's because Goodreads will notice and will be more likely to recommend your book(s) to people who have books in that genre on their shelves. That could be thousands of people Goodreads will recommend your book to – without charge!

❖ However, do be careful about spamming. It isn't acceptable to bombard people with suggestions or fake questions that are designed to get them recommending your book.

❖ Go through your recommendations and see if you can work out which book(s) have been recommended to you based on one of your own books. Then recommend that book(s) to your friends. Once that is on their To Read shelf yours is more likely to come up as a recommendation.

❖ Goodreads makes recommendations based on each of your shelves. Create a shelf for each of your books/genres, and related genres.

❖ Update your Favorite Genres regularly. Make sure that the genres you write in are on there, and any closely-related genres as well. The more you have in your Favorite Genres, the more recommendation shelves you will get.

❖ It is possible to recommend books to others and for people to recommend books to you.

SUMMARY OF SECTION ONE

I
T WILL TAKE YOU just an hour to go through Section One and do all the necessary things you need to get started on Goodreads. Just an hour to get comfortable with Goodreads and get your basic author profile up and running.

That's an hour well-spent.

The steps again are:

- ❖ Sign up for Goodreads as a user – add contacts, select genres, rate a few books, find your way around.
- ❖ Sign up as an author, either by claiming your book or by adding it.
- ❖ Spruce up your author profile, add your blog, add video if you have any. Once your profile is up you can go back to add more things later, just make sure you have a presence for you with, at least, a blog.
- ❖ Learn about profiles and bookshelves.
- ❖ Make some friends, join some groups. Respond to messages and friend requests if you get them, and be sure to thank people for connecting by clicking SEND A MESSAGE on their profile page and sending a quick 'Thank You' without a 'Buy my book'.

Once you're comfortable on Goodreads you can move on to discovering the various ways you can use it to promote your book(s).

SECTION TWO

USE GOODREADS TO PROMOTE
YOUR BOOK

THE WAYS TO USE Goodreads to promote your book(s) are numerous and powerful. They can be as simple as chatting to other users and mentioning your book in groups, to the more advanced - setting up [free] giveaways, and paying for advertising.

Get to know the site first, become an active user, then get going on this section.

If your books are only in eBook format at the moment, it is well worth getting some POD (print on demand) copies, just for the massive benefit of being able to offer them as giveaway promotions.

If you are traditionally published and your publisher isn't making the most of Goodreads for you, do it yourself. Buy a few copies of your books to offer as a giveaway - you will need to run it by the publisher first but they are unlikely to object.

Giveaways are powerful and exciting, but they aren't the only way to promote your book.

Let's look first at reviews ...

CHAPTER 11

ALL ABOUT REVIEWS

REVIEWS ARE THE CATALYSTS for author success – whether on Amazon, Goodreads, or elsewhere. Make your number one goal the gathering of reviews for your books. The more you get, the more likely people are to add your book to their shelves.

Don't forget that, while people can't buy your book on Goodreads (which is a good thing, it makes the site more independent and trustworthy), they can click on a link to buy it from an external sales site (such as Amazon or Kobo).

One of the *huge* benefits of Goodreads reviews is that they are also syndicated to dozens of ecommerce and library catalog sites.

If you have a large number of reviews on a book, it will come to the attention of the Goodreads algorithm and you will start to appear in [relevant] lists when people click Recommendations.

Get even more reviews and you could even appear in the main book suggestions when people join Goodreads. They are usually populated by top selling books, by celebrities and mass-market authors but it is possible to reach those dizzy heights with a book that is selling well and has a large number of reviews.

Don't be tempted to pay for reviews – on sales sites or on Goodreads. Authors can quickly become the latest publishing joke by being found out for doing this. John Locke is a good example. He caused quite a scandal when someone found out that he had paid for 300 reviews for his books. It is a shame that his name is (hopefully temporarily) tarnished because his books are enjoyable and his advice to authors quite sound.

Buying reviews could be viewed as Indie authors just using tricks that traditional publishers have always used. After all, traditional publishers send print copies of books out to reviewers, newspapers, magazines, etc.

Buying reviews, though, is expressly against Amazon's terms and conditions and could get you thrown off the site if you are caught doing it.

Simply not worth it.

If you have already paid for reviews, don't panic. Stop doing it, and encourage authentic ones in future.

Goodreads aims to have reviews that, "remain the best and most authentic in the world". They also list a number of helpful reasons why you should aim to get reviews on Goodreads:

- ❖ Reviews help new readers discover you/your book. Every time someone on Goodreads adds your book to their shelves and/or reviews/star rates it, their friends on Goodreads – and possibly their friends on Facebook – will see that. They could be tempted to add it too.

- ❖ They help readers decide to read your book. It's happened to most of us, you see what looks like an interesting book on Amazon or another book seller and, if it has no reviews, you click away (unless it's free or very newly published). It is a bit like seeing an empty restaurant and assuming the food or service must be bad – so going next door to the busy one.

- ❖ Goodreads reviews work harder for you. Well they would say that but it is true. Goodreads syndicates reviews to: ecommerce sites, library sites, USAToday.com. Your book review could appear on USAToday.com!

HOW TO WRITE REVIEWS

Goodreads prides itself on its users writing honest opinions about books – and welcomes passion.

The site gives the following examples of what they allow in reviews:

- ❖ Creativity. Use the book's inspiration to write a personal essay or piece of creative writing.

- ❖ Images. No nudity or violence allowed.

❖ Pre-publication reviews. Goodreads recognizes that people do receive advance copies of books to review. Therefore they allow reviews as soon as the book is in their database.

Goodreads strongly discourage:

❖ Harshly critical reviews. Criticism is fine if done with eloquence! Saying, "The writing is absolute rubbish, this book deserves to be in a dumpster," doesn't help anyone. Saying, "While the prose could have done with a bit more work …" is more helpful.

❖ Being critical of the author themselves. Mentioning the author is fine but alluding to their behavior, financial habits, social life, or appearance isn't.

❖ Reviews that attack other reviewers. This can be tempting to do actually! I have seen 1 Star reviews of excellent books and I want to write that the reviewers must have been reading the wrong book. Not allowed though.

❖ Self-promotion. "This book is almost as good as my book!" would be deleted pretty quickly.

❖ Hate. Threats, bad language, bigotry are all – quite rightly – disallowed by Goodreads. That's what makes it such a nice place.

❖ Spam. Spammers crop up everywhere, but as soon as spam is brought to the attention of the Goodreads librarians, it is whizzed off where it belongs to a great black hole.

❖ Commercial reviews. Like Amazon, Goodreads doesn't allow reviewers to accept payment for writing reviews. In fact, if you win a giveaway and write a review, you are required to state that in your review.

HOW TO ENCOURAGE REVIEWS

❖ The number one way is to schedule a Goodreads Giveaway.

❖ Join groups, interact with other users and authors, review other people's books – they will often return the favor. Some of the groups also have links to users' blogs, which are a great way to get reviews elsewhere. One of the new ones is showing a lot of promise, Top Of The Heap Reviews. He also does author interviews and giveaways. You can apply to ask for your book to be reviewed on the blog.

❖ Post excerpts of your books (use the author dashboard to add excerpts to your Goodreads blog or post them in relevant group discussions). It gives people a 'feel' for your writing and the chance to sample it before buying.

❖ Post coupons or information about free promotions.

- ❖ Use Goodreads widgets on your website. The widget makes it easy for people to click through and write their review.
- ❖ Ask for reviews. Not in a desperate, pleading way, but perhaps a post on your blog saying that your book is now on Goodreads and you'd love it if the people who mean a lot to you (your blog followers) would find the time to write a quick review of it on Goodreads.

GOODREADS' REVIEW GUIDELINES

Goodreads *does* allow authors to review their own books! It won't be as influential as an independent review but it can give readers an insight into your motivation for writing the book, back story, inspiration, etc.

Commenting on negative reviews is a huge mistake. Goodreads requests that you don't, saying: "The only positive reaction to a negative review is to ignore it".

Goodreads also says that a few negative, or at least not glowing, reviews can actually help book sales as they come across as real and "lend validity to the positive reviews on the book".

REVIEWS
IF YOU'RE IN A HURRY

- ❖ Goodreads reviews are even more valuable than Amazon reviews because they are syndicated to ecommerce and library sites.
- ❖ Every time someone on Goodreads adds your book to their shelves, reviews it, or star rates it, their friends on Goodreads – and possibly their friends on Facebook – will see the news in the feed.
- ❖ Encourage reviews through use of widgets, giveaways, and group participation.
- ❖ Don't respond to negative reviews and don't be tempted to thank everyone who shelves, rates or reviews your books (you could be marked as a spammer).
- ❖ Click LIKE on good reviews.

CHAPTER 12

PROMOTE FREE EBOOKS
ON GOODREADS

I F YOU ARE IN Amazon's KDP Select program you can choose to offer your eBook for free download for up to 5 days in any 90-day period.

Giving away your book may sound counter-productive but bear in mind the principle of loss-leaders in supermarkets. They will sell products at a price that doesn't bring in a profit, in order to get customers in, make sales of other (more profitable) products. A loss leader will often be used to get customers to a particular area of the store, so they will be tempted by other products.

Large companies and manufacturers have used the principle of loss leaders. Wikipedia cite the Gillette razor company, which sells razor handles at a loss in order to sell more of their very profitable razor blades.

The Edison Gas & Electric Company used loss leaders in order to encourage new subscribers for their electricity – they actually gave away electric lamps. Edison is a good example of another way of using loss leaders – to promote a new company or service.

Microsoft's X-Box console was sold at a loss in order to promote game sales. They did this because the game console market already had big players when Microsoft decided to join. It obviously worked, the X-Box now ranks alongside the PlayStation.

As digital authors, giving books away is a risk-free way of turning a tried and tested traditional marketing practice to our advantage. Free eBooks:

❖ Promote you as an author – your 'brand'.

❖ Get your name in front of people who would otherwise not have seen it.

❖ Get your book's name (and, importantly, cover) seen by hundreds (perhaps thousands) of people.

❖ Give people an opportunity to try a new author before buying – if they like one book they are more likely to buy others you have written.

❖ Raise your rankings on Amazon. Their algorithm isn't made public but my own experience and that of other authors suggests that numbers of free downloads does *temporarily* affect bestseller rankings. There are Free and Paid bestseller rankings. Obviously you will rise in the Free rankings during a period of offering your book for free download, but you should also see a rise in the Paid rankings afterwards too. Paid sales tend to increase after a giveaway – simply because your book has been more visible to more people – so your Paid ranking would increase a little, but it seems that rankings rise exponentially more after a free promotion.

❖ Increase the chances of getting reviews. Reviews sell – on Amazon as well as on Goodreads. The more reviews you can get on Goodreads, the more chance you have of your book being listed in Recommendations and Suggestions when people join Goodreads.

So giving your book(s) away is far from being a daft idea. Here are links to a few blog posts from authors talking about their (successful) experiences with KDP Select free promotions:

http://mayalassiter.com/2012/03/my-amazon-kdp-select-free-experience-or-how-i-gave-away-8500-books/

http://davidgaughran.wordpress.com/2012/02/24/why-giving-away-thousands-of-free-books-is-a-good-thing/

The Goodreads Giveaway is not available for eBooks, so you can't use that, but you can use other ways of promoting your Amazon free days on Goodreads:

PROMOTE YOUR FREE DAYS

Adding anything to your author profile means that the update can be seen by everyone you are connected to (friends with) on Goodreads. If any of those people then add your book to their To Read shelf, all their friends will see that.

ADD AN [AUTHOR PROFILE] EVENT

Adding an event is a way to get your book noticed. Don't be disappointed if you don't get many replies, it will have been SEEN and some of the people will have clicked over to Amazon to download it.

Here's how to add an event to your author profile:

- ❖ On the Goodreads main screen, click your photo at the top right-hand side. It will take you to your Author Profile page.
- ❖ Scroll down to your Events and click ADD AN EVENT.
- ❖ Enter the details and click SAVE at the bottom of the page.

For the physical address, I have tried using Amazon's corporate headquarters address in Seattle and no-one has complained!

On the next screen you are given the opportunity to invite people to your event. You can choose from existing Goodreads friends, Facebook friends or type in names manually.

Note that you have to have allowed the Goodreads Facebook app to post to your wall if you want to invite Facebook friends. You can do this from the Invite page by clicking INVITE next to a friend's name and then clicking GRANT PERMISSION on the popup that appears.

You will then be asked to ALLOW the Goodreads Facebook app to post to your wall. This is fine – you can remove permission at any time. I'm not wild about this feature. It puts a post on your friends' Facebook walls that can look a bit dodgy. There are a few friends I don't mind sending these to (because I know they understand it isn't a scam!) but I certainly wouldn't send them to everyone.

On the Goodreads friends tab there is the option to add all, or add within a certain distance (great for signings but obviously not relevant for virtual events). These are much 'safer' as Goodreads people love books!

I usually add all and add a personalized message along the lines of this one:

> **Hi! My [genre] eBook [book name] is free on Amazon today and tomorrow. This is the last free promotion to boost the book's bestseller ranking ahead of the paperback release next month.**
>
> **I would be enormously grateful if you would add the book to your 'To Read' shelf on Goodreads as well as download it.**
>
> **If you do read it, I hope you enjoy it and [e.g. fall for the main character, learn how to ...]**
>
> **Michelle x**

Remember to ask people to download it AND add to their shelves. You want to do everything you can to raise your book's profile in the hope that the Goodreads robots will spot it!

The event will appear on your own profile and in updates:

This is how my activity looked to someone viewing my profile on an iPhone.

The activity shown above resulted in 8,000 free downloads. Prior to using Goodreads, I hadn't had more than 4,000 downloads in any one promotion.

ADD THE DETAILS IN YOUR GROUPS

All Goodreads Groups have rules – do be careful to follow them or you could be forcibly ejected from the groups you have offended! I find the easiest thing to do is to watch and learn for a few weeks after joining a group. You will soon get a feel for what the moderators encourage and what they won't tolerate.

Have a look for authors and readers groups, plus groups in your genre(s).

Go to GROUPS and search for suitable groups. Click on a group name and, on the right-hand side of the screen, there should be a link to their DISCUSSIONS.

If there are posts about giveaways, join in or start your own thread.

The Goodreads Authors/Readers group is good and there are a few threads about giveaways.

In each case, you need to scroll down to the bottom of the screen to find the COMMENT box, where you can add your own message.

Here's how:

Scroll down to the bottom of the screen and look for the COMMENT BOX.

Just above it should be a clickable link called ADD BOOK/AUTHOR, click on that. Type in your book's name and click SEARCH. When it appears click ADD and it will appear in the Comment box.

Add some more information and click POST.

You can choose whether or not to add the post to your own Update Feed by clicking the checkbox. It is possible to deselect the notifications option – so you won't be bombarded with other people's messages on the thread – by clicking EDIT.

It is a good idea, though, to comment on other people's comments, all part of the community feel of Goodreads and it puts your name and profile picture around.

Everyone in the group has the chance to see your message – possibly thousands of passionate Goodreads readers!

PROMOTING FREE EBOOK DAYS
IF YOU'RE IN A HURRY

* ❖ Add the information about your free days to your blog.
* ❖ Mention it in relevant discussions in your groups.
* ❖ Add an event to your author profile.
    * ❖ Go to your book's page on Goodreads and see if anyone has added it to their To Read shelf. Send it to them as a gift.

CHAPTER 13

GOODREADS GIVEAWAY
PROMOTIONS

THERE HAS BEEN A move away from print and towards digital books for a while and it is common to hear authors – Indie authors in particular – discussing the pros and cons of actually having print books at all now.

Well here's one outstanding reason to have your books in print – either print-on-demand or traditional – so you can schedule a Goodreads Giveaway.

A giveaway is a competition – often, but not solely, used by publishers and authors to promote a book pre-launch – to win a paper or hardback edition of book. Goodreads doesn't allow eBook giveaways so a print copy is essential to take advantage of this opportunity.

It is totally free to offer a book as a giveaway on Goodreads – which is a fantastic opportunity ... if you have printed copies of your books. eBook-only authors are at a disadvantage here.

Such is the value of a Goodreads Giveaway that I would go so far as to suggest signing up with a print-on-demand company such as Amazon's CreateSpace just to get a few copies to offer as a giveaway on Goodreads.

Goodreads publishes statistics from time to time on their blog about the results authors have had from giveaways. They are very, very impressive. They show charts over time of the number of books added to Goodreads shelves and there is always a very large spike during a giveaway – and afterwards.

GIVEAWAYS ARE FOR ALL [PHYSICAL] BOOKS

There is a myth that giveaways are only allowed for unpublished or recently-published books – that's not the case. The book could have been previously published. You do have to state the publication date in the giveaway and you have to assure Goodreads that you will be supplying new copies of the book, not second-hand ones!

Goodreads states in the blog that giveaways help kick-start book discovery. Once people know about your book they can add it to their shelves, review it, recommend it, and hopefully discuss it in groups. Some of the huge book successes of recent times started their upward trajectory with a Goodreads giveaway or two.

The beauty about a book being discovered on Goodreads is that people often have their Goodreads settings set to automatically update their Facebook profiles. As the average Facebook user has over 200 friends, that is putting your book in front of a lot of people.

Go to **www.goodreads.com/giveaway** to see the current contests.

You will see that you can sort the contests into:

- ❖ Ending soon.
- ❖ Most requested.
- ❖ Popular authors.
- ❖ Recently listed.

We all like freebies and I know many people who visit the Giveaway page every day! The only downside is that many of the books are only available to people in the US, Canada, Great Britain, and [less commonly] Australia. It is worth scrolling through and clicking on the MORE link next to 'Countries Available' for each book. Some are available worldwide.

When you visit the Giveaway page yourself, you should be shown books that are available to win in your own country. To reach the maximum number of people possible, consider offering the giveaway for your book worldwide. The chances are that the winner will be in the US anyway so the postage costs shouldn't be too expensive.

It is possible to choose giveaways to enter by genre or by searching. Goodreads tailors the results of searches in Giveaways to the person's country – they have the option to override this and select All (presumably if they have contacts in other countries).

Click ENTER TO WIN next to the book(s) you are interested in and enter your address if you haven't already. Click SELECT THIS ADDRESS then click the checkbox to agree to the terms & conditions. You can also choose to add the book to your To Read shelf at the same time. Then click ENTER TO WIN.

As an author you can see straightaway how this could benefit you. LOTS of people enter these contests and the fact that they have done so will appear in their profile updates, as well as on the update page of all their friends. That gives people the ability to click on the link to enter the competition themselves and therefore inform all their friends about it – which could end up with thousands of people entering the competition to win your book, and it ending up on thousands of To Read shelves.

This is much better than Amazon's free lists, which are fairly buried within the site – you have to be actively looking for them to find them. On Goodreads you don't even have to visit the Giveaway page but you will see when friends have entered and you have the ability to click on not one but five links from their entry to go to:

- ❖ Friend's profile page.
- ❖ Giveaway page for that book.
- ❖ Goodreads page for that book – where there will be a link to the contest.
- ❖ The book's author's Goodreads page – to see what else she/he has written.
- ❖ The book's giveaway page.

Giveaways are a brilliant idea. I believe it is worth getting your book into print just for the ability to set up a giveaway on Goodreads. It will put it in front of a lot of people.

You (or your publisher) are responsible for sending the book(s) out to the winner(s) but what's a few bucks postage compared to the usual cost of advertising?

Goodreads states that the average giveaway attracts *825* entries.

You can run an additional giveaway for the same title at another time – in fact Goodreads recommends it. They suggest one before publication and one a few months later, after publication.

They recommend starting the buzz about a book up to six months before its launch. Tim Ferriss uses this technique very well with his books (the 4-Hour series of books: *4-Hour Chef, 4-Hour Body, 4-Hour Work Week*). He builds buzz and sends out hundreds of review copies pre-launch, so that when the book is published, the reviews appear online that same day. It is a very successful strategy.

HOW TO LIST YOUR BOOK FOR GIVEAWAY PROMOTION

Go to the New Giveaway page at **www.goodreads.com/giveaway/new** and enter the following details:

- ❖ Start date.
- ❖ End date.
- ❖ Book release date.
- ❖ ISBN/Book ID.
- ❖ Description.
- ❖ Number of copies to give away.
- ❖ Publisher URL [optional].
- ❖ Countries you are willing to ship to.
- ❖ Tags (to help your book be found in searches).
- ❖ Comment – include who you are, who you work for, and your mailing address. This is so Goodreads can be confident that you will send the free books. If you are an Indie author you may have to assure them in some way that you will send the books. (They don't share your mailing address with site users.)
- ❖ You can check a checkbox to indicate that you are prepared to include a preview eBook (in EPUB format) for people to read. This is a great idea – like the Sample Chapter facility on Amazon.
- ❖ Check to indicate that you agree to the terms & conditions.

Goodreads has a 'Goodreads Giveaway' widget that you can use on a website or blog. You can also link to the giveaway page for your book via Twitter, Facebook, LinkedIn, etc.

If you are enrolled in KDP Select, which gives Amazon exclusive rights to sell your book for contract periods of 90 days, you may think you can't have a paperback edition at the same time. You can if you use the POD (Print On Demand) company CreateSpace. Amazon own CreateSpace so, not only do they 'allow' you to have a paperback edition as well as a Kindle one, they encourage it. They will list your paperback quickly too.

Having a paperback edition can give the Kindle edition a sales boost as the paperback will generally be more expensive, thereby making the Kindle edition seem like a good deal.

GOODREADS' TIPS FOR SUCCESSFUL GIVEAWAYS

Start early Run the giveaway at least one month before publication. Some publishers start as early as three months before publication. If you're already published, go ahead as soon as you like.

Run the giveaway for a month This is the perfect amount of time to let plenty of people enter the contest.

Offer as many books as you can Goodreads recommends giving away at least 10 books. They estimate that around 60% of people review the book they win – a pretty good percentage. Therefore, they argue, the more books you can offer the more reviews you are likely to get. As reviews sell books, this is a very valuable thing to spend a little of your marketing budget on.

The idea is that a proportion of the people who receive one of your books free will be so delighted with their freebie (much more valuable than a free eBook in most people's eyes) that they will review it. Not everybody does, though. So offering more than one book increases the chances of reviews.

However – I have spoken to authors who say that the number of entries to a giveaway contest does not seem to be affected by the number of books on offer. So if you can only afford to order one POD copy, order one and offer that as a giveaway, with a nice note/card to say you hope they enjoy it and you would be tickled pink if they would review it.

There's nothing to stop you running a second (or third) giveaway later on when you have built up some royalties.

Give away signed copies People love signed books.

Run more than one giveaway The most successful books have followed Goodreads' recommendations and scheduled two giveaways – one before publication and one after.

Goodreads suggests running a giveaway for a period of at least two weeks. Again, some authors have had success doing this while others swear by short giveaways because they then appear on both the Newly Listed and the Ending Soon lists! Not a bad idea but personally I'd rather go for a longer timescale, just because of my experience with KDP Select free promo days.

A one-day Kindle promo doesn't have the time to build momentum. I've had most success with three-day promos. I'd be tempted to go for a two-week Goodreads giveaway and see how it goes.

Think like a marketer Your book cover is going to be the first thing to catch users' eyes, then the description. It has to really draw people in and make them HAVE to read your book.

Then they'll not only enter the competition, they'll also be more likely to add your book to their To Read shelf.

Use an advertisement It is possible to buy advertising linked to your giveaway. Giveaways with ads attract 45% more entries than giveaways without ads.

Use the Giveaway widget The Giveaway widget is great for putting on your website/blog so more people can enter the contest. It becomes available to you once you have scheduled a giveaway.

A giveaway can have a snowball effect, starting small and gaining momentum as it rolls. Use all the resources available to you to promote your giveaway.

AFTER THE GIVEAWAY

Once your contest has closed, Goodreads will inform you who the winners are, together with their addresses and links so you can contact them. Be sure to contact them digitally to say congratulations – it will appear in the update feeds – and that their book is on its way.

You really don't want complaints so send the books as soon as you get their addresses.

It's a nice idea to include something in the package – perhaps a 'Thank You' card to say thanks for entering. This is a good idea because hopefully they will put the card somewhere obvious and it will remind them that they need to read and review your book.

GIVEAWAY TERMS & CONDITIONS

* ❖ You agree to supply the indicated number of books on the date the giveaway ends.
* ❖ Goodreads will list (for free) the giveaway book on the giveaways page.
* ❖ Goodreads will collect interest in the book, and select winners at our discretion. Our algorithm uses user data to match interested users with each book.

❖ After the giveaway stop date, click the name of your giveaway (listed under "your giveaways" on the main First Reads page) to see the list of winning addresses. You will also be emailed a list of winners. You are responsible for shipment of the books. Failure to do so will result in us not inviting you over for cake ever again.

❖ You agree to not store the winners' mailing addresses and to never mail anything to the winners except the indicated book. This is important. Privacy rules and all that.

❖ Winning users are encouraged but not required to write a review of the book they receive.

❖ eBooks are not allowed. Every winner must receive a physical copy of the book – as soon as possible after the close of the contest.

How To Win Goodreads Giveaways

In the Giveaway terms & conditions, they state that:

'If more people are interested in a book than there are copies available, we will pick the winners at our discretion. The factors that go into our algorithm are: randomness, site activity, genre of books on your shelves, current phase of the moon and more.'

They aren't without humor, these Goodreads people!

Now if we bear in mind that we as authors are offering our books as prizes in order to increase the likelihood of getting reviews, we can trust that the Goodreads algorithm is more likely to give them as prizes to people who have previously reviewed other books.

Therefore you are more likely to win books if you are active on the site, write reviews, and participate in discussions.

Have plenty of books on your shelves, read multiple genres (especially your own – have LOTS of books on your shelves in your own genre (s) and review, or at least star, plenty of them), and be active on the site.

Isn't that wonderful? Not the prospect that you may win a book (although that's never a bad thing!) but the thought that readers are discovering this too. They are realizing that the more reviews they write and the more books they have on their shelves, the more they are likely to win giveaways. Yay! Happy author dance.

GIVEAWAYS
IF YOU'RE IN A HURRY

❖ Giveaways are free – both to enter and to set up. That means *free* advertising, seen by *millions* of people.

❖ You have to have print editions of your books available to give away – Goodreads suggests 10 copies minimum but don't let that put you off if you can only afford to offer one copy.

❖ Run a number of giveaways if you can. Try scheduling one before publication (if appropriate) for about a month. Then try another one after publication, running it for just a few days. This was you will pick up the people who search for giveaways 'Ending Soon' as well as giveaways 'Recently Listed'!

❖ Indie Authors: Put your book on CreateSpace – you can do that even if you are enrolled in KDP Select. Amazon own CreateSpace so that means your paperback will be listed alongside the Kindle edition. The Kindle edition will appear to be good value as it will probably be cheaper than the paperback, and you may see an increase in sales of your Kindle edition. You can also have CreateSpace send out the winning copies direct to the winners if you wish.

❖ The idea behind giveaways is for winners to review the book they receive. Most authors report between a 30 & 50% review rate. That's an out-of-the-ballpark better percentage of reviews after a promotion than you would get on Amazon with KDP Select free days.

❖ Giveaways increase awareness about your book. The average giveaway gets 825 entries. That's your book being in front of 825 new eyes AND all their friends' eyes. Priceless. That can be increased to over a thousand entries if you can afford to support the giveaway with a self-serve advert (see the next chapter).

❖ Find giveaways in the dropdown menu under BROWSE on the main navigation or go to: **www.goodreads.com/giveaway**

CHAPTER 14

ADVERTISE ON GOODREADS

WHEN BROWSING ON GOODREADS (a good way to waste a few hours!), you may notice some ads around the site. Not too much actually, to their credit, which makes the ads that do appear more engaging.

There are some usual Google-type ads and there are 'Sponsored Books'.

A full launch campaign costs a couple of thousand dollars, so it's something of a considered purchase!

Goodreads also offers pay-per-click advertising options, where you can select demographics and genre preferences. They call this their 'Self-Serve' advertising. It is quick and easy to set up.

Paid opportunities to advertise on Goodreads can include ads on:

- ❖ The Facebook app.
- ❖ Mobile apps.
- ❖ The Goodreads home page.
- ❖ Quizzes.
- ❖ Special 'New Releases' mail-out.
- ❖ Banner ads.
- ❖ Sponsored links.

❖ Paid spots in the monthly newsletter that is sent out to all users (those who haven't unsubscribed). That goes to millions of users – it has a larger circulation than Time magazine!

When you consider that Goodreads is browsed mainly by people who love reading, an ad on Goodreads is potentially much more cost-effective than a general Google ad or even a more targeted Facebook ad (currently running cheaper and more effective than Google ads but they are still fairly expensive).

Goodreads has a (US) rank of 58 on Quantcast[3], who report it as having a massive 8 million page views per day. Quantcast shows that Goodreads' visitor demographics are very interesting – mainly adult and female, many are parents, most have been to college or grad school. If your target market is similar, Goodreads may be a good place for you to try some advertising.

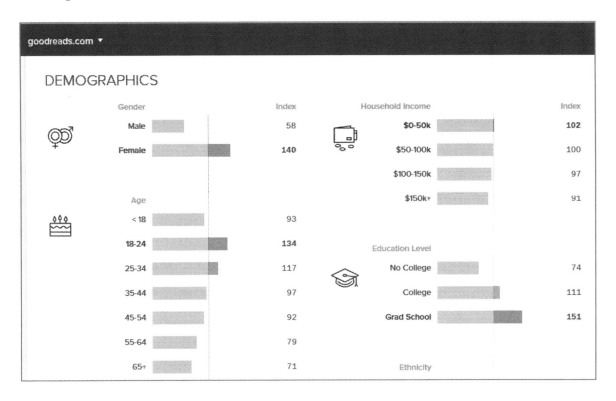

---

[3] Quantcast.com is a fascinating site. You enter the URL of a site you want to know more about and it will show you details about that site's visitors. Very useful information if you are thinking of advertising on that site or submitting articles.

The thing that shocked me most about the demographics is that the majority of Goodreads users are **less** affluent than the average Internet user. So this is a good place to promote free and low-price books.

It does make you wonder how all these college-educated people are managing to be less affluent than the average Internet user – perhaps they are mainly teachers! In that case, if you have written books for children, or on how to manage on a small income, Goodreads is *definitely* the place to advertise!

I think demographics are a handy tool but they aren't set in stone so I wouldn't let the less affluent thing put me off advertising an expensive book on Goodreads.

Looking at the existing adverts, it is clear that the site is held in very high regard by traditional publishers, with ads appearing regularly from the big name publishers,

The Goodreads advertising program is aimed at authors and publishers but they do accept [select] adverts from other interested parties as well (for example eReaders, editing services, proofreaders, etc.). They have worked with all the major publishing houses but aren't anti-Indies, seeing them as the next evolution of publishing.

SELF-SERVE ADVERTISING

Goodreads is trialing what they call self-serve advertising, which I have tried and found easy to use. Like Google AdWords, you enter the information yourself that you want to appear on your ad.

Like Facebook ads, you can choose who gets shown your ads. So you can target people who have read and highly rated specific authors (you would choose authors in your genre or who write in a similar style to you), people within a certain age range, male or female, or specific genres.

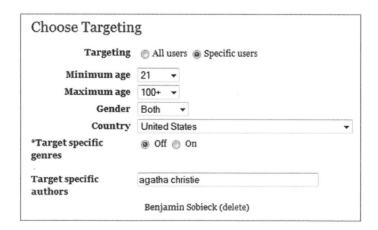

Choosing genres brings up the familiar Goodreads genre box, which Goodreads does recommend when targeting ads.

Then the fun begins – adding authors. I have found a method that works for me, it might work for you ...

HOW TO CHOOSE AUTHORS FOR TARGETED ADS

❖ Find a book similar to yours. If you don't know of one, go to Amazon and click on your book's page. There will be sections called, 'Customers who bought this item also bought' and 'What do customers buy after viewing this item'. Go through the books and read their descriptions, you should be able to find something similar to yours.

❖ Next, go back to Goodreads and find that book (or multiple books, if you have found more than one) and see if they are on any lists in Listopia. If they are, bingo!

❖ I chose a number of books that came up in my Amazon search, as well as one I already knew about, 'I, Jack' by Patricia Finney.

❖ Go through the lists and add the authors to your targeting for your ad. It is worth writing them down for next time. Not all authors will be on Goodreads, so have a big list so you can hit a good number.
The better-known authors will get better responses. I'm a big fan of Dodie Smith, who wrote the original '101 Dalmatians', but she didn't write many books and died in 1990, so is unlikely to have a big enough following on Goodreads to make it worth my while only targeting people who have rated her books.

This method will ensure that you don't waste money by showing your ad to people who are unlikely to be interested in your book (but who may click on it just to read the description.

That click, which is unlikely to result in a sale or shelf add, will cost you - which is why it's called Cost Per Click advertising).

You decide where to send people who click on the ad – the book's Goodreads page or perhaps a sales page (Amazon, Kobo, etc.). Goodreads recommends sending people to the Goodreads page, saying that this has maximum viral effect. That means that people are more likely to add it to their shelves (whether they buy it or not), which will then be seen by the Goodreads friends and possibly their Facebook friends as well (the average number of friends on Facebook is around 200 so this aspect could boost your campaign tremendously).

```
Set Your Budget

Billing

Daily budget:  $ 8.00      (minimum: $1) ?

Bid amount:  $ 0.70      per click
Suggested bid: $0.50 - $151.53
Higher bids ensure that your ad gets shown first.
The average bid on the site is .50.

How long do you want your ad to run?

Run my ad for  1        days          11 total clicks (11 clicks per day × 1 d

☐ Auto renew this campaign after 30 days      Total amount: $8.00

We only offer auto-renew for 30 day increments.
If auto-renew is enabled, your credit card will be charged for an additional 30 days when funds
If you adjust your daily cap or bid, the auto renewal amount may change.

When do you want to your campaign to start?

◉ now
○ later

When do you want to your campaign to end?

◉ automatically, when you run out of credit
○ on a specific date

What is my total bill?

Total amount: $8.00
```

So if you want to go for viral effect – books on shelves, ratings, and reviews – then linking to the book's Goodreads page makes sense.

However, linking to the book's page on, say, Amazon, would mean that an immediate purchase is a little more likely. If you are going for immediate sales rather than a sustained campaign, a sales page link makes more sense.

When I worked freelance, I ran several Facebook advertising campaigns for clients. I know from that experience that sending people to an external site from an ad cost more than sending them to a Facebook page. I don't know if the same is true on Goodreads as I haven't done a wide enough variety of advertising campaigns to analyze the data yet. I suspect it may be the case though.

After setting up your ad(s), you just enter credit card information and then the ad will go for approval to Goodreads. Once they have approved it, it will go live (if you chose to start it 'Now'). They typically take two working days to approve ads, so don't expect 'Now' to mean right away!

You will be billed for the campaign total and that will be entered as credit on your Goodreads advertising account. The credit will then reduce on a Cost Per Click (known as

CPC) basis, which means that every time someone clicks on the ad, your bid amount will be taken from your credit.

Duplicate clicks from the same person are not counted.

Goodreads doesn't guarantee to hit your daily budget every day – your campaign will be extended is the budget isn't spent. This may be because there are a lot of advertisers competing for space, or it could be because you have chosen authors that don't have many fans rating and reviewing their books.

Goodreads states that if your campaign delivers more clicks that you purchased you won't be charged for them.

When the campaign is running, and afterwards, you get access to statistics. These show how many people viewed your ad, clicked on it and how may added your book to their shelves.

If you can't see your ad on the Goodreads home page it may be because you haven't shelved or rated books in the genre you have chosen. It could also be because you are over your daily budget – check again after midnight.

How To Run A Good Advertising Campaign

Goodreads recommends this strategy for running a good advertising campaign, which is based on running two ads at the same time, to test results.

- ❖ Schedule two ads, using the book's Goodreads page as the landing page.
- ❖ Target about 5 genres with the first ad if you can.
- ❖ Target 8-10 comparable (well-known) authors with the second. It is important to target authors with high ratings.
- ❖ Ideally, use the ad to promote a giveaway. The average giveaway gets around 825 entries, but a giveaway supported by an ad campaign attracts a whopping 1,292 people!
- ❖ Include a call-to-action such as: 'Add to your shelf', 'Enter to win', 'Read an excerpt'.
- ❖ Click the checkbox 'Engagement Stats' on the sign-up page for ads and you will be able to track and analyze the entries.
- ❖ Enter a bid amount. This is like Google AdWords and Facebook ads. You can buy Goodreads ads from 10c per click. The average is 50c per click. There is a minimum spend of $1.00 per day and you can run a one-day campaign.

The self-serve advertising page is at:

www.goodreads.com/advertisers/new_ad

You can also go to: **www.goodreads.com/advertisers** and fill in their form to receive a media kit.

SELF-SERVE ADVERTISING
IF YOU'RE IN A HURRY

❖ You set the budget so you don't need to worry about getting in too deep. Set a small daily amount to see how it goes.

❖ Target using your own genre and similar authors. Try different ads to see what works best.

❖ Remember the demographics – Goodreads has a high proportion of women and Caucasian people, who are slightly less affluent than the average Internet user. This isn't the best place to advertise a $90 coffee table book to black male CEOs.

❖ Use the ad to promote a Giveaway – you will get more entries.

SUMMARY OF SECTION TWO

৵৽

THE VARIOUS WAYS TO promote books on Goodreads are very effective, mostly free, and don't require a massive input of time.

The steps again are:

❖ Reviews – writing reviews doesn't have to take lots of time, and it demonstrates participation and commitment to the site. The more you write, the more your name can be seen around the site, and the more likely people will be to click on your picture and check out your profile and books. 'Give to get' was never more appropriate than on Goodreads.

❖ Promote free Kindle days – use events, groups, discussions, your blog, and general chatting.

❖ Giveaways – Goodreads Giveaways are so effective that it is worth getting some POD copies if your book is only currently in eBook format. Schedule two giveaways, one pre-launch (if appropriate) and one after. Otherwise just schedule giveaways a few weeks or months apart (depending on your budget). Offer anything from one copy to 10 each time. Giveaways get results - they get reviews, they get ratings, they get your book on people's shelves, and they prompt more sales.

❖ Advertising – If your budget allows, support your giveaway with a self-serve advertising campaign (or a standalone self-serve campaign, even without a giveaway).

You can also contact Goodreads for a media pack:

www.goodreads.com/advertisers

SECTION THREE

OPTIONAL EXTRAS

❧❧

Get to know these when you have time.

CHAPTER 15

NEWSLETTERS

Unless they unsubscribe, all users receive the monthly [email] newsletter. There are also specialist newsletters for people interested in Young Adult and Romance.

Sponsorship (advertising) can be bought for advertisements in the newsletter – the main ones being the banners at the top and bottom of the newsletter, and sponsored books, which appear in the right-hand column.

The newsletter is worth reading. It has author interviews, featured books and groups, quotes, trivia, and quizzes.

I haven't seen any independent reports of how successful advertising is in the newsletter so can't make any recommendations. What I would say is that the banner adverts I have seen have been very professional, leading me to believe they are traditional publishers (as well as other, related companies, such as Sony's Reader Store).

That does suggest that newsletter advertising is effective - many traditional publishers are struggling, they wouldn't waste their money if it didn't pay off for them in extra sales.

The newsletter archive can be found at:

www.goodreads.com/newsletter

There is also an excellent Author Newsletter:

www.goodreads.com/author/newsletter

It isn't published as often as the user newsletter – just a few times a year – but it has some useful writing tips, and advice on how to get the best out of Goodreads.

You can read the archives at the links above.

CHAPTER 16

GOODREADS WIDGETS

I F YOU HAVE A website – especially a WordPress-run site – you are probably familiar with widgets. You can do this easily add a new widget yourself by adding a new TEXT/HTML widget in APPEARANCE > WIDGETS and pasting the text right in.

For the non-technical, it is just a small piece of code that you can give your web designer to add to your site.

Professionally-designed and maintained sites are great but many people prefer to do their own sites. WordPress is very easy to get to know if you fancy having a go yourself. All you need to do is buy some hosting (from $5pm) and a domain name (around $11pa), then download the free WordPress software. A site can be up and running within a couple of hours.

I recommend downloading an inexpensive but comprehensive eBook called *WordPress Your Way* by Nancy Hendrickson. It will walk you through the whole thing from buying the domain name, installing WordPress, and tweaking it to get the best out of it. Running your own site doesn't have to take a vast amount of time and it puts you in control. You can then see the analytics to see who is visiting, where they come from, how long they spend on the site, which are the most popular pages, etc.

Having a WordPress site means that you can add Goodreads widgets in seconds. They are worth adding for a number of reasons:

1. Increased social proof

Anyone can call themselves an author. If you add one or more Goodreads widgets on your site you are proving that you are a published, authentic author. This raises your site's authenticity in the search engine's eyes.

Have you tried Googling your own name? Unless you have an unusual name, the chances are that your site won't appear on the first page of the SERPs (Search Engine Results Pages). Being on the first page is very important – when was the last time you clicked through to page 20 of the SERPs when you searched for something? I'll go to maybe page 2 or 3 but if I don't find what I'm looking for I change my keyword terms and search again.

If you have any books published, the first result is likely to be Amazon. Amazon generally gets very high ranking in the results. If you are an author, a Google search for your name should find you on page 1 of the SERPs just because of Amazon.

The next results tend to be the social networking sites that Google holds in high regard: LinkedIn and Goodreads. Then possibly pages from your own site. My sites have ranked because of all the links pointing at it from my Goodreads and LinkedIn profiles. That's social proof.

When Google, Bing, or another search engine looks at your site to decide where to rank it in the page results, it will see that lots of sites are linking to it (Amazon, Goodreads, LinkedIn, etc.), so it raises it in the results over another site with a similar name that is without multiple incoming links.

Get it? Social proof is not only important, it is valuable. Online advertising is expensive. I hate to think what I would have had to pay to rank in the top three of Google without the links coming in from my social networking profiles. Thousands of dollars. I could have paid an SEO company to get my site ranked but it would have cost nearly as much (the results would have lasted longer though).

When I ran a training company some years ago I had to pay over $2,000 to get my site ranked quickly.[4] That's a lot of money. For authors, marketing money would be better spent – just a fraction of it would be necessary – on Goodreads advertisements that directly promote your book(s), rather than your site generally.

---

[4] Now I know a little about SEO I would choose to create a few YouTube videos instead. YouTube videos rank very quickly on Google.

2. Improved visibility on Goodreads

Anything that will get more people to Goodreads, and to your books, raises the possibility of more people finding you on Goodreads, which could lead to big success.

3. Make it easy for readers to find you

Authors used to hide behind agents and publishers, now we have to be more visible and more available. Readers like to be able to interact with the authors they follow, they want to be able to ask questions, make suggestions, or just say 'Thanks for a great read'. I know I do! I love being able to comment on a book on Goodreads and have the author reply – it's a great feeling, and it happens a lot on the site.

Adding a Goodreads widget to your website makes it easier for Goodreads users to connect with you – it's a simple click rather than having to go search. I have found that people often join Goodreads after seeing a widget on an author's site, which is great.

I wish I had got to grips with Goodreads earlier than I did. A local reporter wrote an article about me when my first children's book, *Mo The Talking Dog*, was released. The article mentioned that my books were available on Amazon. My website analytics (data that shows who has been visiting your site) showed that lots of local people had Googled my name, and visited my site or my Amazon links. But then I lost them – I don't know what happened to them.

If I had put Goodreads widgets on my site, they would have been able to find my Goodreads profile rather than the bland Amazon links. The profile would give them the opportunity to read my blog, watch a video, ask questions, write a review, and/or add my books to their shelves. All these things would have helped the chances of others finding my books.

If that same person had Googled my name or my book's name, not only would they have found the Amazon links, they would also have found my website. They may well have seen the Goodreads 'Add Book' widget and they could have simply clicked it to add it to their Goodreads shelves (or to join Goodreads and then add it). Then ALL their Goodreads friends (often hundreds of them) would have seen that they had added my book and might have been tempted to take a look at it themselves.

If any of those Goodreads users were using the Facebook app, their updates would also be added to their Facebook Timeline, potentially putting my book in front of another couple of hundred people. Ah hindsight!

HOW TO USE GOODREADS WIDGETS

Go to your author dashboard by hovering on your profile picture on Goodreads. From the dashboard, select AUTHOR WIDGETS.

They can each be configured to fit in with your website. Then all you have to do is copy the code and paste it into a Text/HTML widget on your site. If you don't have a WordPress site, ask your designer to handle it for you. A quick copy and paste shouldn't cost much.

BUTTONS

These are simple icons that you can configure and add to your website next to any mentions of your book(s), to encourage readers to add it to their Goodreads shelves.

REVIEWS WIDGET

This is great for showing off your best Goodreads reviews. You can actually choose the type of reviews you want to feature.

You need to click the Reviews Widget's ADD TO WEBSITE button from the widgets page and it will take you to a section where you can configure the widget.

You can choose:

- ❖ The number of reviews to show.
- ❖ The minimum star rating.
- ❖ The widget's title as it will appear on your site.
- ❖ The colors and size.

If you have your own style sheet (CSS) on your site you can link to that so the widget will look more like the rest of your site (don't worry if you don't understand CSS, it isn't essential).

Then all you have to do is copy the code that appears on the page and paste it into your website – or send it to your designer.

As we know that reviews help sell books, it makes perfect sense to have your Goodreads reviews showcased on your website or blog.

To prevent this book from being overly-long for busy authors, I haven't included the detailed instructions for how to configure and add widgets to websites. There is a step-by-step video in the course that I mention at the end of this book if you need some help.

ADD TO MY BOOKS WIDGET

This is a widget you put on your site that gives others the opportunity to add your book to their Goodreads shelves without leaving your site. Great for keeping people on your site and for getting your visibility higher in Goodreads all at once.

The other big advantage of this widget is that it shows people which of their friends on Goodreads have added your book. This is HUGE. People are influenced by their friends and are much more likely to add your book to their shelves if one of their friends has already done so.

BOOKS WIDGET

This gives you a simple way to display your books, together with their average Goodreads rating and number of reviews.

Of course you can do this with a monetized Amazon widget but if you are actively promoting yourself on Goodreads, perhaps with a giveaway and some advertising, using the Books Widget on your website would be a good idea. The more people who see your profile and books on Goodreads the better because that creates a 'To Read' snowball.

GIVEAWAY WIDGET

This only becomes available after you list a book as a giveaway with Goodreads. It is a fantastic little piece of marketing to put on a site/blog.

You could also indirectly use it on other social networking platforms, by tweeting/updating: 'Visit my site to enter a contest to win one of my books', followed by a link to your site.

CHAPTER 17

LISTS

❧❧

LISTS (ALSO CALLED LISTOPIA) are the Goodreads version of Amazon's Listmania. People create lists, add their favorite books, and others vote for books' positions on them.

These – like Listmanias – are a little-known, untapped source of traffic and SEO back-up. They are very powerful for book promotion.

Anyone can make a list and add relevant books to it. Lists are available for everyone to read – and are indexed by Google and other search engines.

Lists are great for finding popular and mid-list books on Goodreads. Lists are a great place for Goodreads users to find books to add to their To Read shelves.

Lists tend to have very specific titles – so not '20th Century Fiction' but 'World War II Fiction'. Not just 'Animal Books' but 'Talking Animal Books'.

Find Listopias from the BROWSE dropdown menu on the main navigation bar at the top of every Goodreads page or go to: **www.goodreads.com/list**

There will be featured lists, lists with recent activity, lists friends have voted on, and more.

They are a little like groups, in that they are laid out in types, can be searched, and are also sorted by tags.

There is an opportunity to add any book on Goodreads to a list that you have created, or to vote for it on someone else's list.

LISTOPIA TIPS IF YOU'RE IN A HURRY

❖ Get your book(s) on some lists – create a couple yourself and vote on others in your genre. You often find people add your book to their lists after seeing it on others. Lists are a good way to get your book in front of people.

❖ Vote on lists – especially in your genre. Get your profile picture out there, people may click on it and find your books on your profile page.

CHAPTER 18

GOODREADS APPS

APPS ARE A GREAT way of maximizing your use of social media while reducing the amount of time you spend on it. For example, you only have to update Goodreads and your Facebook profile is automatically updated. It saves you time and increases your exposure.

They are also great for making use of time that would otherwise be wasted. I do a lot of my social media while commuting or waiting for appointments. If I have a morning meeting, rather than battle rush-hour traffic and struggle to park my car, I will set off early, avoid the rush, get an easy parking place, and spend some time on Goodreads (often in my groups).

FACEBOOK

Log into Facebook and type GOODREADS in the search box:

Then click on the Goodreads App. There may be others, including impersonators. The Goodreads one will have a large number of users.

The Goodreads app looks a little different to many other Facebook apps. The only thing you can change is who sees the update – your friends, public, just yourself. I haven't found any security problems and am happy to use it myself so I do recommend it. If you ever do have problems with it you can remove it and stop it having access to your account by going to your Account Settings on Facebook.

I have set mine for Friends because I don't like personal things appearing on my Facebook profile (which I use for keeping in touch with friends and family so could contain holiday photos, photos of my children, etc.).

Click either VISIT WEBSITE, or SEND TO MOBILE to install the app, which gives it permission to update your Timeline with your Goodreads updates.

The app will update your Facebook status (with your permission) when you have finished reading a book, reviewed books, or updated your Goodreads status.

A useful thing is that Facebook lets you know when you have followed someone on Goodreads. You can then click on their name and follow them on Facebook if you wish.

Goodreads offers you the chance to tell your Facebook contacts every time you do something, but it is very easy to click or unclick the checkbox.

IOS

The Goodreads app is available on the iTunes store:

https://itunes.apple.com

It makes checking into Goodreads quick and easy and is a great way to tap into what would otherwise be wasted time, such as when commuting or waiting.

The main features are:

- ❖ A barcode scanner – this is brilliant! You scan a book and the app recognizes it and offers to add it to your bookshelves.
- ❖ Respond to friend requests.
- ❖ Read book reviews and friends' updates.
- ❖ Recommend books to friends.
- ❖ Check new books and popular books lists.
- ❖ Read public domain (free) eBooks.
- ❖ Rate and review books.
- ❖ Join online book clubs and groups.
- ❖ See details of any events which are coming up.
- ❖ Share information on Facebook or Twitter.

All very useful. In practice, the barcode scanner is a little tricky to use – you need a steady hand and good light. I usually get my daughter to scan books in for me! The app is tremendously useful though, especially when travelling.

The reviews of it are interesting. Readers obviously value it for keeping 'To Read' lists and for keeping track of what they have read.

ANDROID

The Android app is available from Android apps on Google Play:

https://play.google.com/store/apps/details?id=com.goodreads&hl=en

It looks different, of course, to the IOS app but behaves in much the same way, with a barcode scanner and links to groups, books, your profile, your friends, and updates.

CHAPTER 19

CREATIVE WRITING

THE CREATIVE WRITING SECTION of Goodreads is a fairly new one. You can find it under the Community menu on the navigation bar. It became large and popular surprisingly quickly.

The Creative Writing section gives **all** Goodreads users the chance to upload samples of their writing. There is a very large fanfiction[5] element to this section. That's something to consider if you have any favorite books you would like to write some backstory about!

I was surprised to see Goodreads encouraging fanfiction but I'm guessing they see this section as competition for FanFiction.net and Wattpad and it looks like they're onto something. The fanfiction section is very popular. Some big-name authors allow and encourage it (notably JK Rowling and Stephanie Meyer) while others are strongly against it (particularly Anne Rice and George RR Martin). If you are considering exercising your fiction muscle with a little fanfiction, be prepared to do some research first to check that the author allows it.

This section is a very useful place to do some market research. You get to see which stories are popular and which aren't. If you're thinking of writing about vampires, the Goodreads Creative Writing section should be the place you go to right after you check out Amazon to

---

[5] Fanfiction = writing written by a fan of, and featuring characters from, a book, movie, TV series, etc.

see whether that genre is still selling. The popularity of free writing won't be a good indication of what people may be prepared to pay for but it's very indicative of what is on trend and whether or not it may be worth including some vampires or werewolves or whatever in your next book. Many people would guess the whole vampire genre to be long past its sell-by date but it's still riding high in the charts and the popularity stakes.

It's not just for fiction – the nonfiction section is popular too and useful for the same purpose. Test the waters with some nonfiction writing in this section, see what catches people's attention. I used to do this with the site HubPages. I would add articles on there to see which topics were popular. I knew the popular ones were worth developing into something saleable.

Even just a glance at the categories can give you a good idea of what's popular at the moment (Science Fiction & Fantasy). Writing a short story for this section could be a great way to gauge how much interest there would be in a full-length book on the same topic as Goodreads users can 'like' pieces of writing and comment on them.

Authors who contribute to the Creative Writing section get a section on their profiles that shows what they have written. Fans can jump straight to their writing, in the same way they can go to their books. This gives us a huge opportunity to showcase our writing.

While I wouldn't argue for wasting too much of your time penning stories or articles that can never be published, it isn't a bad idea to dip a toe in the waters of the Creative Writing section. You can find new fans there who may not otherwise have come across your work. You might also discover a flair for writing in a genre you hadn't considered before.

So, if you're inclined, make the most of the Creative Writing section by:

❖ Having a go at some short stories, articles, or even fanfiction (only if you're a novelist – your fanfiction fans aren't likely to buy your nonfiction books).

❖ Reading other authors' pieces to see what's popular and working for them.

❖ Keeping an eye on the popularity of categories that you may consider writing in or incorporating into your books.

❖ Keeping an eye on rising and falling trends.

CHAPTER 20

WHAT NOT TO DO

A QUICK SCAN OF [SOME] authors on Twitter will reveal what not to do on social media. The worst offenders simply scream 'Buy My Book!' at anyone and everyone. Others only interact with other authors and yet their tweets are all about their own books, so are intended for potential readers. That is something to guard against very carefully on Goodreads.

Goodreads is, at the moment, still somewhat under-used by authors. That's a great thing because it means it is still mainly populated by the people we love, admire, and yearn for ... readers. Using Goodreads properly can give us opportunities that can't be found elsewhere – especially at no or low cost.

However, there are a few things we need to be aware of.

FRIENDS

- ❖ Don't only friend authors. You are naturally going to have a large number of author friends but don't deliberately only seek to friend authors to the exclusion of other users.

- ❖ Readers are the lifeblood of Goodreads, friend them, chat to them. Don't abuse them. Don't see them as cash cows. Respect their views and reviews, even if they are negative about your book. Never, ever respond to negative reviews.

- ❖ Don't thank people for positive reviews – an occasional 'like' is fine though. Goodreads doesn't recommend it. There's a good reason for that. If you thanked everyone, Goodreads would be alerted to you as a possible spammer – as you would be sending out multiple similar messages, which would appear in your updates.

GROUPS

❖ Don't spam fellow group members, follow the rules.

❖ Don't forget to read the rules of every group you join - they are all different as they are set by the moderators, not Goodreads.

❖ Don't join lots of groups without participating in them. Choose a small number and be active in each (it doesn't take long). Smaller groups are better for getting to know people well. Genre-specific groups are brilliant if it is something you are passionate about, you will find others who are as well. Book club groups choose a book for everyone to read together and discuss – these are great. If they are in your genre, even better, as they may pick your book to discuss.

RECOMMENDATIONS

❖ Don't send out lots of recommendations and ask those people to recommend your books to their friends. Recommending books to others needs to be done infrequently, if at all. I can find books for myself, I can pick them right off your shelves, I don't need you to stick them under my nose.

ADS

❖ Don't buy an expensive advertising campaign and then create the ads yourself. The Goodreads ad program can be very effective, if done well. If you are doing a couple of sponsored ads, go ahead and try them out, but don't try to create ads for a big campaign yourself – hire a specialist. Giveaways are different, you can write the copy yourself but an advertising campaign is going to cost. There's no point investing money in a campaign unless you are going to have a great ad to point people to.

❖ Don't use just one self-serve ad. Try several, they are inexpensive. Try different targeting tactics - genre, age, other authors rated, etc., and use different wording in the ads. This is known as split-testing and it works. Once you find an ad and target combination that works, throw everything you can at it.

APPS

❖ The apps are great, really useful, but you may want to be a little careful. The Facebook one in particular sets my teeth on edge. I did something one day that filled my Facebook news stream with dozens of posts from me on my friends' walls. I was horrified and spent a long time laboriously going to every friend's page to delete them. I loathe spam, we're all busy enough without having to wade through unwanted messages. Now I'm careful to uncheck the checkbox to post to Facebook on most of my posts. I don't mind people seeing updates on my own page when I have finished reading a book but I don't want to put posts on all my friends' pages about every little thing I do on Goodreads.

CHAPTER 21

SUMMARY

THE EASIEST WAY TO fall in love with Goodreads is to start using it. Armed with the knowledge you have gained from this book, you won't be wasting your time.

People sometimes complain that they find Goodreads difficult to navigate. Once you have found your way around, you will (hopefully!) wonder why you ever thought it was difficult. It's just a giant database of books and the people who love them.

The piece of writing advice that is most often given to writing newcomers is, 'Read, read, read'. I'd like to update that to: 'Read ... then talk about the book(s) on Goodreads'.

It is vital to see Goodreads as a place to talk about books, to interact with other readers, and to discover new books and authors. Try not to see it merely as a place to advertise your books or to post a message about your upcoming free days. It is SO much more than that.

Goodreads is exactly what is says on the tin – it's a place to find good things to read. That happens because readers talk to other readers and recommend books. Become a Goodreads reader and people – the right people, who will do great reviews - will naturally be drawn to your books.

Good luck – I hope to chat to you on Goodreads ... right after I've finished reading the novel I've been neglecting since I started writing this book!

IF YOU DON'T GET ANYTHING ELSE
OUT OF THIS BOOK, GET THIS!

GOODREADS PRESENTS A TRULY amazing opportunity for us as authors – too good an opportunity to consign it to the 'Must get round to it' bin.

There are some phenomenally successful authors who are on Goodreads – still interacting, still engaging their readers and potential readers.

This is what they do and what you can do, very easily:

❖ Claim your author profile.

❖ Add your blog or start a Goodreads blog.

❖ Add books to your shelves in your own genre (s), and others. Add at least 20 books so you can use the Recommendation Engine.

❖ Check your Recommendations page. Find the book(s) that have been recommended to you based on books you have written. Add these to your To Read shelf and get your friends and family to do so as well. People who have those books on their shelves are more likely to get your book(s) recommended to them.

❖ Join a few groups and interact with other members.

❖ Update Goodreads in some way at least a couple of times a week – the more often you do, the more you are likely to be seen. Do this by, for example:

❖ Updating your Currently Reading book (just add a new page number, it's that quick!)

❖ Add some books to your To Read shelf.

- ❖ Add some books to your Read shelf (ones from your childhood if you haven't read many books recently).
- ❖ Update your blog.
- ❖ Interact in a group.
- ❖ Add a video to your author profile.

And the most important, most book-promotingy thing you can do on Goodreads:

- ❖ Schedule a Giveaway. If you only have an eBook currently, order one print copy to give away (via a POD publisher). It is worth it.

I know the pain of the early days, of seeing your book sales figures seemingly stuck like the broken hand on a clock – and I know the joy of looking on Amazon and seeing that magical orangey 'Bestseller' banner next to your book.

Life for authors is something of a rollercoaster – we have to expect extreme highs and extreme lows. But as the highs get higher, the lows get less low (terrible English, I do apologize!).

I'm not yet selling hundreds of books a day. Most of the time I'm still selling single digits on some books and double digits on others. I feel a wonderful sense of excitement, though, at the possibilities that Goodreads brings now that I know it well. You can too.

I would wish you luck but you don't need it. Not anymore. Use Goodreads and you won't be leaving your success to luck.

FAQ
& TROUBLE-SHOOTING

❧❧

Is Goodreads Suitable For Nonfiction Books?

Absolutely. There are numerous groups and genres for nonfiction books.

How Do I Change My Profile Picture?

There are two – your user profile picture and your author profile picture. Your user picture appears at the top-right of any page, as a thumbnail. Your author profile picture appears as a larger picture on the left-hand side of the page when people click on your name anywhere on Goodreads.

Change your user profile picture by clicking on the little arrow to the right of your profile picture thumbnail at the top-right of any page and selecting EDIT PROFILE.

You will see your profile picture on the right with a link underneath it to change/delete it.

Click EDIT MY AUTHOR PROFILE and there will be an option to EDIT/REPLACE the photo (or add it if you haven't already).

Be sure to scroll down the page to SAVE any changes you make.

You can tell which profile you are editing by the link that will be on the right-hand side of the page. If you are on your author profile it will be EDIT MY USER PROFILE and if you are on your user profile there will be an EDIT MY AUTHOR PROFILE link.

Where Is My Author Dashboard?

Click on your profile picture on the right-hand side of the Goodreads home page or go straight to:

www.goodreads.com/author/dashboard

You will find great statistics on your dashboard, showing you your book numbers (shelf adds, ratings, reviews – even who is currently reading your books!), and your own statistics.

How Do I Add An Excerpt From My Book?

Go to your book's page and click EDIT DETAILS and UPLOAD AN EBOOK on the next page.

Then choose the file and, if it is the full manuscript, decide how much (percentage) you want to make available for people to read and whether or not they can download the sample or have to read it in their browser.

Click SUBMIT when done.

This is a great way to give people a chance to sample your writing.

Where Are The Widgets?

They are a bit hidden! Go to EDIT PROFILE by clicking the dropdown arrow next to your profile picture thumbnail at the top-right of the Goodreads navigation bar. You should be on a page called My Account. Click the WIDGETS tab just underneath the page title.

If you aren't on My Account, click EDIT MY USER PROFILE and you will be taken there. The Giveaway widget doesn't become available until you schedule a giveaway.

Can I List My Pen Names Under My Author Account?

Not really. Goodreads suggests adding your real name as a second author on the books written using a pen name. Either that or have two accounts (see below).

CAN YOU HAVE MORE THAN ONE GOODREADS ACCOUNT?

Yes, it isn't like Facebook where you can be thrown off the site for having two. In fact, Goodreads says you can have an account for each penname you use as they don't have a facility for listing pen names under one author account.

CAN YOU BUY BOOKS THROUGH GOODREADS?

No. It's a social network, you don't have to worry that if you click 'Add Books' you are buying them.

You can click links to take you to external sales sites though. There are 'Book Links' on each book's page to take you to the likes of Amazon, Kobo, etc.

Readers can read some books on Goodreads itself - free books, classics, and books by authors who have been dead for over 50 years. There are tons of wonderful books available to read. There are also free eBooks to download on Goodreads. Go t:

www.goodreads.com/ebooks

and click DOWNLOAD EBOOK. These tend to be the newer books. Some authors post 'shorts' or excerpts from paid books as well.

DO YOU HAVE TO JOIN FACEBOOK TO JOIN GOODREADS?

No. The link between Facebook and Goodreads is there to make it easier for people to log in to Goodreads (a Facebook account also enables you to log into lots of other sites as well as Goodreads), and to enable people to use the Goodreads Facebook app.

HOW DO I READ/DOWNLOAD EBOOKS ON GOODREADS?

Go to:

www.goodreads.com/ebooks

There are generally two options – Read Book or Download eBook (or excerpt). If you click Read Book the book will open up onscreen in the Goodreads eReader. If you click Download eBook you will be sent to a new page with options to download the book in (currently) either Txt or Mobipocket/Kindle format.

If you click on Download next to Kindle you will get an Open or Save File popup. If you are using a computer (not a mobile) you can choose to open the book with the Kindle app and read it right there on the screen. If not, you can save it and transfer it to a Kindle.

There is an option to Manage your eReaders at:

www.goodreads.com/ereaders

so you can select the ones you have on your computer.

The options are:

iBooks	Kindle for PC
Kindle for Android	Goodreads IOS App
Goodreads Android App	Calibre
iPad	Kindle for iPad
Kindle (all types)	Nook
Adobe Digital Editions	Google Books
Aldiko (Android)	Kobo
Kobo apps (IOS & Android)	Sony Reader
GoodReader	eReader
eReader on iPhone	MobiPocket Reader
FBReader (various platforms)	Bluefire Reader
Moon+ Reader (Android)	Pandigital

Most of these apps/eReaders are free – find them in your device's store.

HOW DO I FIX PROBLEMS WITH THE FACEBOOK APP?

Be careful about deleting the app from Facebook – it may prevent you from being able to sign in to Goodreads using Facebook.

People can be concerned about spamming their friends if they use the Facebook app. One solution is this: When you first start using the app, it will ask you who you want to be able to see the posts it makes for you on your timeline. Choose ONLY ME.

They will appear on your profile but you can easily and quickly delete them. If you want some of them to be public, or visible to friends, click the privacy icon that appears on the post and select the option you want.

How Do I Add The Goodreads Tab To My Facebook Page?

Facebook profiles and Facebook pages are different things. Your profile is the one that you may want to keep private but your page(s) can be much more public, which you want if you are promoting and your books.

Log into Facebook and type GOODREADS in the search box, then click on the Goodreads app. When you get to it, don't click GO TO APP, click on the little arrow next to the settings cog and click ADD APP TO PAGE.

Select the page you want to add it to and click ADD APP TO PAGE.

Then click on the app (you may have to click the dropdown arrow as it will be underneath existing apps if you have them installed) and choose the settings you want to show – your author page, a group page, or your books.

How Do I Add A New Bookshelf?

Click on MY BOOKS at the top of the main Goodreads screen.

On the left-hand side, below the names of your existing shelves, click ADD SHELF.

A box will appear directly below where you just clicked, click in it, type in the name of the new shelf, then click ADD.

How Do I Change The Name Of A Bookshelf?

Click on MY BOOKS at the top of the main Goodreads screen.

On the left-hand side, above the names of your bookshelves, there is a title 'Bookshelves'. Click EDIT to the right of the title.

The names of shelves you have created can be changed – click RENAME to the right of their names.

The three pre-existing shelves, Read, Currently Reading, and To Read, can't be changed.

How Do I Change Which Shelf Is Featured At The Top Of My Profile?

Click on MY BOOKS at the top of the main Goodreads screen.

On the left-hand side, above the names of bookshelves, there is a title 'Bookshelves'. Click EDIT to the right of the title.

Here you can click in the FEATURE radio button of the shelf you want featured at the top of your profile.

If you write in one genre, have a shelf for that and feature it. If you write in more than one genre you can have the shelf featured that contains the book you are currently promoting.

I Can't Log In To Goodreads

If ever you can't log in – either manually or using Facebook/Twitter, etc., try logging out of anything else you are logged into.

I couldn't log into Goodreads manually once and it was because I was logged into a different Gmail account. I think Goodreads thought I had a split personality and didn't want to deal with me!

I Have An Author Profile On Goodreads But I Didn't Add It

When your book is listed on Goodreads an author profile is automatically created for you. You need to claim it in order to use and update it.

Click on your name then scroll to the bottom of the page. There should be a line saying 'Is this you?' followed by a LET US KNOW link. Click the link and Goodreads will assign that profile to you.

How Do I Contact Goodreads?

Go to:

www.goodreads.com/about/contact_us

It will come up with helpful suggestions, depending on what you choose as the subject of your enquiry. If you scroll to the bottom of the page, there will be a box to type in and submit.

Email for Goodreads support:

support@goodreads.com

How Do I Become A Librarian?

Librarians keep things running smoothly on Goodreads. They do a lot of good on the site. They help correct inaccuracies, add missing data about books, such as covers, edit book and author information, combine separate editions of books (to help aggregate reviews/ratings), and more (such as preventing legal problems by making sure any necessary citations are present).

Once upon a time on Goodreads, everybody had an advanced version of a standard user account. They could add their own book covers and do other administrative-type tasks. However, misuse, simple messing-up, and Amazon's decree that their site can't be used for copying images, meant that things had to change and a new breed of Goodreads user was born: librarians.

To become a librarian, all you need to do is have a minimum of 50 books in your profile, then you can apply by going to:

www.goodreads.com/about/apply_librarian

There is a helpful Librarians Manual on the site so you can get an idea of whether you would like to take on the role. There's a fair bit to it but you only take on tasks that you are comfortable with.

I have found librarians to be very quick and efficient.

Librarians Manual:

www.goodreads.com/librarian_manual#everyone_librarian

APPENDIX 1

SUGGESTED GOODREADS SCHEDULE

I WROTE AND USED TO teach a course called, 'Manage Your Social Media In Under 10 Minutes A Day'. It was for small business owners who felt that they didn't have the time to have a professional presence on Facebook, Twitter, and LinkedIn. It was effective. Most people stuck to the schedule and managed to fit it in to their busy schedules.

When you run a small business you are often responsible for advertising, marketing, public relations, book-keeping, customer relations, human resources, sales, and emptying the bins. It is hard to fit everything in. It's a little like being an author. Even if you are a traditionally-published author, with a big money publishing house behind you, you are still piloting your own ship. The publisher will only promote your book for a certain period of time, after that it's up to you to keep the momentum going. You have to do some of your own marketing, at least, if you are going to prevent your book's destiny being the local bookstore's bargain bin.

Indie authors have to do it all themselves and they are more like small business owners. As authors we know that we need to avoid the quick and desperate 'Buy my book' messages but we don't want to waste time on trivial, non-productive chit-chat. It is hard to strike a good balance between the two.

It is possible to have a presence on social networking platforms without it sucking up a huge amount of time but it does take a large amount of self-discipline! I believe Goodreads gives us an amazing opportunity to create a presence that will draw readers – without it eating into our writing time.

Here's a possible schedule for you to promote your own books, interact with readers, attract potential readers, and network with other authors:

Daily

❖ Check notifications – respond to any that are asking questions or offering to review your books.

❖ Respond to friend requests (it's just one click).

Twice Weekly

❖ Update your status – e.g. 'Working on first draft', '5% of the way through *War & Peace*', etc. It is quick and easy to update your reading progress. Click on the UPDATE STATUS link next to the book on the home page. Add a different page number, add a message, or click I'M FINISHED.

❖ Check your groups and respond to posts, reviews, etc.

Once Weekly

❖ Write a review of a book – or use some you have written before (I have lots on Amazon to transfer, they just need some re-wording). If you are in any author groups it is good to review each other's books but throw in lots for authors you don't know as well (e.g. newcomers, celebrities, classics).

❖ Add new books to your shelves. You need a range of books on your shelves (books automatically go on your Read shelf when you review them), and you need to be sure to read and review books in the genre (s) you write in.

As often as possible

❖ Update your 'Reading Now' list with the % (eBooks) or page number.

❖ Add new content to your author profile page – a blog post, video, new favorite quotation.

When You Release A New Book

❖ Announce it before release and ask for reviewers. Send a copy and swear them to secrecy. Ask them to add the review on Goodreads and Amazon on release day.

❖ Tell Goodreads (enter the ISBN/ASIN).

- ❖ Ask for the cover to be added in the Librarians Group.
- ❖ Add an event for its release.
- ❖ Create a contest/giveaway if it is a physical book.

After Release

- ❖ Add status updates about its meteoric rise up the bestseller lists. Remember to thank your Goodreads friends for their part In that.
- ❖ Keep up your Goodreads interaction while writing your next book.

Combine all this with your other social networking accounts:

- ❖ Post links to reviews, bestseller lists, etc.
- ❖ Post a screen grab of your book's place at the top of the bestseller lists.
- ❖ Post screenshots of any online media coverage and scans of physical newspapers/magazines that feature you/your book.

APPENDIX 2

HOW TO BECOME A LIBRARIAN

LIBRARIANS ARE GOODREADS USERS who demonstrated commitment and activity on the site, and were accepted when they applied for Librarian status. They have more access to the Goodreads database than regular users and can do more.

In the early days of Goodreads, everyone had the sort of access that librarians have now. As they site got bigger there were a few important changes, such as not being able to use Amazon's information for book descriptions and covers, and there was a small amount of misuse and errors. So Goodreads had to restrict what people could do – otherwise they risked the site being broken and/or ending up in court! Now they give people different levels of access to the site. Most users – and authors – have basic access but librarians have a degree more.

To become a librarian you just need to have been on the site for a while and have added 50 or more books to your shelves. Then you can perform some of the admin tasks that are needed around the site.

As an author, if you have just published a book, you will probably need to add it manually to the Goodreads database. Although you can do that, and add basic information, you can't (at the moment) add the book's cover because that requires a higher level of access to the database. So authors need to post a message in the librarians group requesting that their cover be added (with a URL to it). A librarian will pick up that message, download your cover, upload it to the Goodreads database, and add it to your book. It isn't a one-click task, it takes a few steps and librarians do a wonderful (and very quick) job.

There are also super librarians, who have even more access to the database – more to do with being able to delete things that ordinary librarians can't, editing at a deeper level (such as sub-genres of a genre), and merging quotes and quizzes.

Study the Librarian Manual:

www.goodreads.com/librarian_manual

then, assuming you have 50+ books on your shelves, apply at:

www.goodreads.com/about/apply_librarian

APPENDIX 3

RESOURCES

❧ ❧

GOODREADS IS HUGE so it can be hard to find the parts you need quickly when you are looking for help.

These are the first pages to try first:

www.goodreads.com/author/how_to

www.goodreads.com/author/guidelines

www.goodreads.com/help/list/author_program

A lot of problems can be fixed/helped by librarians in the Goodreads Librarians group:

www.goodreads.com/group/show/220-goodreads-librarians-group

There is a massive help section that is fully searchable:

www.goodreads.com/help

PAT FLYNN'S FACEBOOK GROUP

https://www.facebook.com/groups/357112331027292

Pat Flynn is best known for his highly successful Smart Passive Income blog and podcast. He now writes books as well. He started this group as a way to bring together other writers and authors, to share tips, successes and disappointments, and encourage each other.

TOM CORSON-KNOWLES'S KINDLE PUBLISHING BIBLE GROUP

https://www.facebook.com/groups/KindlePublishers

Tom Corson-Knowles is a great example of what Guy Kawaski would call an 'APE'! He's an Author, Publisher, and Entrepreneur. He has a wealth of experience even at age 25. He wrote his first book with his doctor mother and learned the basics of Indie publishing quickly. With his unique experience as an online marketer, he shares book marketing tips that can't be found in other books on writing.

He has published a series called 'The Kindle Publishing Bible'. Just one of them – The Amazon Analytics Bible – helped me to understand that my sales were being negatively affected by my book's description. His tip enabled me to add analytics to my Amazon sales page and I was able to see that I was getting more hits than downloads on free days – a few tweaks to the book's description on the sales page sorted that out. I've also received many valuable tips from other people in the group, which have been both useful and encouraging.

NOVELPUBLICITY

www.novelpublicity.com

NovelPublicity was founded by author Emlyn Chand. The site is packed with useful information for authors and she has written a number of articles on how to maximize your use of Goodreads.

SLIDESHARE PRESENTATION

Facebook Tells You How To Market Your Kindle Book (from Amy Harrop):

www.slideshare.net/AmyHarrop/facebook-tells-you-how-to-market-your-kindle-book

DIGITAL CASE STUDY

http://publishingperspectives.com/2010/05/digital-case-study-can-goodreads-ads-help-unknown-authors-find-an-audience/

This article mentions one author's experience using both Facebook and Goodreads ads. He cancelled the Facebook ads, having won fans but not seen an increase in book sales. The Goodreads ads, however, performed better.

That is contrasted with the experience of another author who had initial success with Goodreads ads but who was out-bid by a rival and saw sales fall off.

BOOK BLOGGERS

A search of Goodreads will bring up some great book bloggers. Here's my favorite of the moment, a new blog that is growing quickly. I particularly love the Saturday Morning Kids idea.

http://topoftheheapreviews.com

This is a great Goodreads group where you can meet book bloggers:

www.goodreads.com/group/show/56962-book-bloggers-of-goodreads

BOOK TRENDS

As part of my research for this book, I researched book trends.

Novels lead the way in earning the big bucks so tend to be the ones heavily promoted, and therefore popular, on Goodreads.

Vampires and other paranormal creatures (werewolves, werecats, shape-shifters, etc.,) have obviously been amazingly popular over the last couple of years and remain so. They are certainly discussed a lot in the Goodreads group discussions.

Dystopian stories – think 'Hunger Games' – are the big thing at the moment and a rising trend.

The new genre, 'New Adult', is becoming very popular. It has its own genre section on Goodreads:

www.goodreads.com/genres/new-adult

It is one of those trends that could explode in the way that vampires did a couple of years ago. New Adult books tend to feature lead characters aged between 18 and 26 who are embarking on independent life.

Shelve books in this genre in order to show your interest, and monitor their popularity. If it's your thing, consider writing in this genre as it looks like a good one.

Genres > Science Fiction > Dystopia

Dystopia is a form of literature that explores social and political structures. It is a creation of a nightmare world - unlike its opposite, Utopia, which is an ideal world. Dystopia is often characterized by an authoritarian or totalitarian form of government. It often features different kinds of repressive social control systems, a lack or total absence of individual freedoms and expressions, and a state of constant warfare or violence. Many novels combine both Dystopia and Utopia, often as a metaphor for the different directions humanity can take in its choices, ending up with one of the tw...more

New Releases Tagged "Dystopia"

APPENDIX 4

FROM THE
GOODREADS BLOG

❧ ❧

THE GOODREADS BLOG IS well worth following. They publish news stories, launches, and statistics that can be jaw-dropping. Here are just a few of their words of wisdom, taken from various posts in their blog over the last year:

❖ Readers discover books in numerous ways on Goodreads (see pie chart). These ways can cross over and cause a ripple effect.

❖ Run giveaways BEFORE publication to build buzz and get some advance reviews.

They say that for one book, Random House ran three giveaways in advance, which garnered enough reviews to get the book Goodreads editorial coverage and placement in the Goodreads recommendation engine.

❖ An advertising campaign can give a book a great boost. They suggest 'well-timed' ads, placed after early publicity/marketing efforts (such as giveaways).

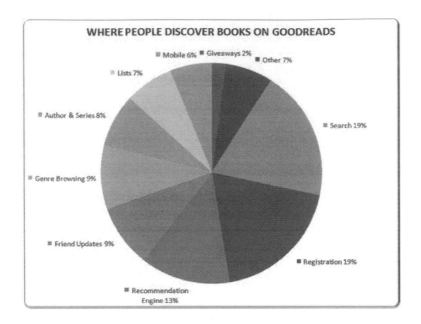

Here is the breakdown of the pie chart Where People Discover Books on Goodreads:

- **Giveaways - 2%**. The best free way to build buzz about a book prior to its launch.

- **Other - 7%**.

- **Search - 19%**. People hear about a book, search for it, and add it to their 'To Read' shelf.

- **Registration - 19%**. When people join Goodreads they are shown popular books to choose from to add to their shelves. Goodreads say this is because, "We want to make sure you see something familiar when signing up, so we show books that many readers have liked". Other methods of discovery are better for finding more obscure books. The average engaged reader adds over 30 books to their 'To Read' shelf during registration.

- **Recommendation Engine - 13%**. Books that make this don't need to be bestsellers but they do need to have **several hundred ratings** (stars and/or reviews) for them to come to Goodreads' notice. Goodreads says, "If you know of a strong comparable title to your book and you are able to market your book to those readers – and they respond by adding your book to their Goodreads account – our recommendation engine will notice this correlation and be even more likely to suggest your book to the right readers". GOLD!

- **Friend Updates - 9%**. The average Goodreads user has 19 friends (actually, most of my 200+ plus friends each have at least 100 friends, many over 300). Goodreads state that 79% users discover books from friends offline; 64% from friend updates on Goodreads.

- **Genre Browsing - 9%**.

- **Author & Series - 8%**. 76% of authors have written more than one book.

- **Lists - 7%**. Goodreads has over 11,000 user-created lists (Listopias), with over 5,000,000 votes. People love lists!

- **Mobile - 6%**.

Goodreads has seen a massive 60% increase in books discovered since they launched their Recommendation Engine.

Goodreads sharing on Facebook is also driving book discovery – with 10 million books being shared per month, generating 220 million impressions per month. Imagine what you'd pay for that using Facebook Ads!

Goodreads states that Twitter & Facebook are not great sources of book discovery (perhaps author discovery though).

APPENDIX 5

CASE STUDIES

FIFTY SHADES OF GREY - EL JAMES

The phenomenon that was *Fifty Shades of Grey* was published on June, 20th 2011. Goodreads' statistics say that there was small spike on the graph, showing that there was a flurry of interest initially, but it then dropped, until it was chosen by a Goodreads Group.

The Romance Readers Reading Challenges Group started reading it on July, 3th 2011. The group has over 4,500 members and 500+ added the book in one day.

Then it received another boost as the Erotic Enchants group started reading it on October, 6th 2011. They have over 2,400 members and 500+ added the book on one day, 600 the next. The discovery spike really started to climb in October 2011.

In November 2011 it was nominated for the Goodreads Choice Award in Romance. 2,500+ people added the book, causing a large spike on the graph.

Then – prompting a large spike of interest – it was on the Today show. CBS News said:

> *"So how did an obscure BDSM novel, which Publisher's Weekly confirmed began as 'Twilight' fan fiction, become a phenomenon? At least part of the explanation can be found in the social network for bookworms, Goodreads."*

Goodreads indeed has a lot to do with the mind-blowing success of Fifty Shades of Grey. Interestingly, EL James participated in a Goodreads chat with a group in January 2012.

EL James remains an active member of Goodreads, with over 5,000 friends, membership of numerous groups, and frequent updates on her profile. She rates books in her own genre, as well as others. Considering that she is one of the most phenomenally successful authors of recent years, her very active participation in Goodreads worth taking note of.

MATCHED - ALLY CONDIE

A giveaway for a single copy of the book *Matched*, a dystopian novel by Ally Condie from Penguin Young Readers, ran in 2010, when the site was smaller than it is now. The winner wrote a glowing, 5-star review on Goodreads and mentioned it in her blog.

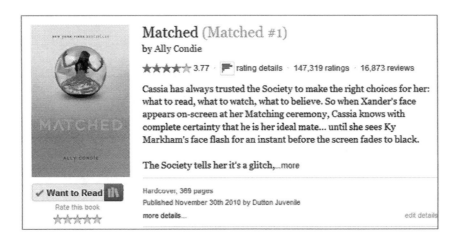

Her friends read it in their Goodreads update feeds, and commented on it. Other people reviewed the book (600 of them), and all BEFORE publication date (they got advance copies).

The book came to Goodreads' attention when another publisher wrote to ask how Penguin Young Readers had managed to get so much attention for the book, pre-release. Goodreads featured it in the 'Mover & Shaker' section of the newsletter, which, "drove a huge number of people to add it to their shelves."

'Matched' became one of the most popular books on Goodreads and remained popular for months afterwards. It has over hundreds of thousands of ratings and thousands of reviews. It is rated at an average of 3.77 stars – further proof that you don't have to have a 5-star book to sell well (*Fifty Shades of Grey* has an average 3.60 star rating).

It is still bringing in a lot of money for the author, with good rankings on Amazon and elsewhere.

BOOK BONUS: EXCERPT FROM *PR FOR AUTHORS*

CHAPTER ONE
WHAT EXACTLY IS PUBLIC RELATIONS?

WHEN YOU READ THE PHRASE 'PUBLIC relations', what pops into your mind? We asked a few people this question and the answers were varied:

- ❖ Marketing/Advertising.
- ❖ Reputation management.
- ❖ Spinning.
- ❖ Sales.
- ❖ Sending lots of press releases.
- ❖ Telephoning reporters.
- ❖ Networking.

One definition often bandied around in media circles is that PR is:

> *"The care and feeding of reporters."*

That was certainly true when I worked in PR in the 1980s – I spent a lot of time buying drinks for reporters! Reporters aren't the only people we want to reach now, though. We're kind of cutting out the middle person with post-Internet PR We do still want to reach reporters but also the many, many bloggers and regular Internet users who will repost interesting content. With modern public relations we are actually aiming to reach the *public*!

Some PR umbrella bodies spend years coming up with a definition of what PR is and it is usually along the lines of promoting a person or company's image and controlling what the media finds out about it.

There's a good definition of the website of Alexander G. Public Relations[6], a Kansas-based PR agency. It says:

> *Advertising buys AWARENESS;*
>
> *Strategic public and media relations earn CREDIBILITY.*

That's a great way of showing the differences between advertising and PR It doesn't matter how much money you throw at advertising if you don't have credibility.

After my first job in PR, I switched to advertising and was one of the account handlers of a large electricity company in the UK. They had a huge advertising budget, which they spent in national press, but they didn't spend much on PR – and it showed. It never ceased to amaze me how much money they were willing to spend on advertising but very little on customer service. Customers would constantly complain about the company's customer service and the company's answer was to throw more money in the advertising budget! If they had diverted some of it to training their customer service staff and some to PR, they would have had happier customers, a better public image, and higher profits.

Let's look at the different aspects – real and perceived - of PR individually.

MARKETING/ADVERTISING

> *Marketing = the activities that are involved in making people aware of a company's products.*
>
> MERRIAM-WEBSTER DICTIONARY

Marketing is PR's conjoined twin – each unique yet intimately linked. They are both concerned with publicity.

---

[6] http://www.alexgpr.com/about/what-we-do

In a company, a marketing department can incorporate the advertising and PR departments or they could be separate – it often depends on the size of the company and its need for publicity.

Publicity means telling people about your product/service, getting the news about it out there by various means. A marketing department might draw up a schedule of promotional activities and then buy in the services of an advertising agency and/or a PR agency to provide those services.

Advertising usually means paid promotional activities – such as advertisements in print publications, on radio/TV, or online ads on Google, Facebook, etc.

PR is generally concerned with more subtle publicity, often involving relationship-building and issuing press releases that provide material for reporters. Sometimes a reporter will respond to a press release with a telephone call to get more information. PR is about being available for that call, forging a mutual-trust relationship with the reporter, and having relevant information available (quickly, knowing that the reporter will be working to a deadline).

Another thing that a marketing department (or the marketing part of an author's brain!) is concerned with is coming up with offers, competitions, and events. As authors, we are used to this with KDP Select free promo days, reducing our book prices for special events, providing free copies for reviewers, book signings (physical and virtual), blog tours, and more. We know that we need to promote these activities or they fall flat.

Every author needs a good marketing plan – a schedule of activities that you intend to do in order to raise awareness of yourself as an author brand, and of your books as individual and series titles.

How Marketing/Advertising Affects You:

Even if you are traditionally-published, you are in many ways responsible for your own marketing. A publisher is only going to spend a certain amount of money and a certain amount of time marketing your latest book – it probably won't do anything to push your back catalog.

Publishing houses don't have the big budgets they used to have anymore and will only lay out cash they know they are going to get a return on. That's why you will see adverts and promotions for the big celebrity authors but not the newcomers or the mid-list ones.

cont/d...

If you are an Indie author, the whole marketing thing is on your shoulders. There is freedom in that, of course, but some pressure too! You have to learn the ins and outs of advertising quickly or you are in danger of wasting a lot of money and sinking without trace.

The bottom line is that *all* authors have to learn how to market themselves and their books. They need to promote their personal brand and build/maintain their reputation.

There are a lot of books out there and a lot of authors telling people about their books. You need to market yourself and your books so that people will find them. You can do that through buying adverts (generally now that will be online, perhaps on Google or Facebook or specific sites), creating offers, alerting promotional websites about those offers, sending press releases, posting on social media, staging a virtual blog tour, or numerous other ways – all under the umbrella of marketing.

There's no point spending money on advertising if you haven't paid attention to PR, though. Yes, schedule some highly targeted ads on Facebook, take advantage of a special offer coupon from Google AdWords, do some Goodreads self-serve advertising to support a Goodreads giveaway, but don't do it without working on your PR as well, or it will be wasted money.

REPUTATION MANAGEMENT

PR guys are often portrayed as sharks on TV and in movies. In the original series of *Dallas*, JR Ewing, the main anti-hero, hired a public relations guru/shark to rescue his oil company's image. He thought that was possible, even though he spent most of the time himself damaging the company's image. PR guys have a tarnished reputation because of this and other stereotypes, which is ironic considering what their job is all about!

People often think that PR is some sort of miracle fix when everything has gone wrong. It's true that a well-oiled PR machine can swing into action to minimize damage after a publicity stunt goes wrong, or a customer complaint is mishandled. It's much better to manage PR well before things go wrong though. Better and less expensive.

That's done through:

> ➢ Providing information for reporters, so they don't have to scrabble around elsewhere to get it and – dare we even hint it? – making some things up!

> ➤ Being very professional and protecting your own brand/image.
> ➤ Being available to answer questions so you can clarify things yourself and not allow people to guess or grasp at half-truths.

Reputation management now is often handled on social media – with varying degrees of success! Some brands and companies do a tremendous job of managing customer service via social media platforms. We'll look at several later.

HOW REPUTATION MANAGEMENT AFFECTS YOU:

As an author, this means establishing your credibility as a 'brand'. It means behaving! It means portraying yourself as you want to be seen – so no tales of drunken nights out on Facebook and no comedy photo on LinkedIn.

Some authors are tempted to jump into reputation management when they get what they consider to be a bad or unfair review on Amazon. It's tempting but something that you should never do. For starters it would make you look like an amateur – professional, successful authors don't comment on their reviews (many don't even read them). It could also risk escalating into a nasty public spat.

There's a reason why celebrities hire PR people to handle their reputations – because most people don't have the skill, tact, or experience to do it themselves.

SPINNING

Max Clifford was a well-known, almost notorious, PR man. He ran a successful PR agency in the U.K. but was best known for promoting dubious news 'scoops'. (He is now better known for being convicted of a series of sexual assaults.)

He started as a reporter and took a job in the press office of EMI records. One of his first jobs was to promote The Beatles, which he obviously did quite well, as they were unheard of before he took over. Let me repeat that – The Beatles had been signed by a record label and had been playing in clubs for years but they didn't become a big hit with the public until the PR machine kicked in. Interesting. Clifford later represented OJ Simpson, Marvin Gaye, Frank Sinatra, Muhammad Ali, and Marlon Brando, among others.

He started on his road to notoriety when he 'spun'[7] a story about a comedian called Freddie Star. The newspaper headline read, 'Freddie Starr ate my hamster' and got widespread

---

[7] Definition of spinning a story = to give a news story a particular emphasis or bias.
Source: http://www.oxforddictionaries.com/definition/english/spin

publicity. The comedian later admitted that the whole thing had been invented to generate publicity for his tour. That was one of the first examples of PR being used to create stories – and to gain money as stories are often sold to newspapers. That's why people sometimes associate PR with lying. PR people try to dissociate themselves from that sort of behavior and say that is the work of publicists. Maybe, but the work of a publicist and the work of a PR person can look quite similar!

HOW SPINNING AFFECTS YOU:

As an author, hopefully this won't affect you because spinning stories generally backfires. The truth comes out eventually and it isn't worth the damage to your reputation to gain some temporary publicity on the back of a lie or half-truth.

Where clever PR gurus succeed, sometimes, is in giving a true news scoop to a reporter or paper in return for them running something about a client of theirs that needs publicity. It's fairly unlikely that you will ever have access to a story that a reporter would consider newsworthy but if you do, you might be able to get them to run a piece about your book as well!

SALES

This is a misconception as PR people aren't sales people. They don't actively hit the streets or the telephones to try to get people to buy things. They are always aware of sales potential though. They will use every opportunity they can to promote their company/client – whether that is at conferences/events, to reporters, in interviews, or other means.

HOW SALES AFFECTS YOU:

If you are traditionally published your publisher will probably have sales people to get bookstores to stock your books. They will try that for a couple of weeks – six at most. Then they will move on to push the next batch of newly-released books. So traditionally published authors need to join the ranks of the Indies who need to keep one eye on sales opportunities at all times. Publishing house salespeople will attend conferences and get to know the book buyers; you can do the same by attending conferences and writing events.

cont/d ...

You can approach bookstores yourself. Often a local, independent bookstore will stock an author's books simply because they are local residents.

You can also network online, via social media. You won't – hopefully – be saying "Buy my book" in the way a salesperson would, but you would be putting on your PR hat and spending time making relationships, getting to know people. That's the way to make sales without being seen to be selling!

SENDING LOTS OF PRESS RELEASES

This is true! They used to be mailed out manually but today it is much easier thanks to the Internet. It is also easier to find suitable contacts to send press releases to.

Press releases are usually commissioned, researched, and then written – often with the help of interviews with relevant people – before being sent. They are then approved before sending out. Sending out means being sent to relevant reporters and editors. The word 'relevant' there is important. They hate getting bombarded with press releases that aren't relevant to them, yet it happens surprisingly frequently.

The U.K. has a national newspaper called the *Financial Times*. It only carries financial news, yet they get press releases about everything from the latest baby product to anti-wrinkle cream. And, no doubt, a few book launch press releases as well. That's fine if the book is a financial one, of course, but most won't be.

Blanket sending of press releases is counter-productive as it makes reporters less likely to read the ones that are relevant to them. Most of us know now how to block out things because we are all assaulted with so much information in the digital age. Reporters are the same.

HOW PRESS RELEASES AFFECT YOU:

Press releases aren't just aimed at reporters, due to much online content now being user-generated. We put our releases 'out there' to be indexed by Google and other search engines. What we really want is to appear on page 1 of the search engine results pages (SERPs) because that is the best way to be found. Few people click past the first page of the SERPs.

cont/d ...

A modern press release is – potentially – available forever online, rather than being a one-day wonder, as used to be the case. Now we can put our releases out via online press release distribution services that will get them indexed by search engines. Then we can post the information everywhere online – via social media, blogs, pings, multimedia, and more.

We still go after reporters, though, because they remain strategically important for publicity. You will need to make lists of relevant publications/media outlets (newspapers, magazines, TV and radio stations) for each of your books and find names of reporters who work for them.

You can just send press releases to 'Newsdesk' or 'Lifestyle Editor' or whatever, but you have more chance of success at building a relationship if you can get a name. You can send your press release to these publications/media outlets and you can also send them to online services – PR distribution services, online news directories, etc. Try to find some reporters local to where you live as local stories often make the news more readily than they do for a national paper/station.

You should also upload your press release to your own online platforms – your website/blog and social media accounts. It's all indexed by Google and provides more social proof that you are who you say you are. It makes your books more discoverable as well.

Much more on press releases later in the book.

TELEPHONING REPORTERS

Many people think that you should follow up a press release with a telephone call. You could … you could also visit a local zoo and punch a hungry tiger on the nose. Neither of those things is a safe idea.

Reporters are incredibly busy people and newsrooms are insane with activity, noise, and deadlines. No reporter will welcome a telephone call from every person who has sent him/her a press release – it would mean being on the telephone all day! Maybe it used to work in the past when money was less tight and newsrooms had more staff. Now, it's unthinkable.

A reporter or editor may want to talk to you after they have read your press release, if your story is of interest/relevance to them. Sometimes it takes longer than that. They may note that you are an expert at whatever and remember you in a few weeks when they're doing a relevant story. All you need to do is make sure you are available and give them lots of ways to contact you.

> **HOW THIS AFFECTS YOU:**
>
> It's great - just send your press releases out. Don't follow them up with telephone calls. There may be occasions when you will need to call a reporter but it won't be just to see if they got your press release.
>
> If there is a news story that is very relevant to your expertise, you may want to telephone the reporter who broke the story, to see if they would like a quote from you for a follow-up story. You could email instead, if you prefer.
>
> Do be very available so reporters can contact you. Give them every method: telephone, cellphone, business and home emails. They will sometimes try to get hold of you with just an hour's deadline for a story, wanting a quote – often at odd times of night!

NETWORKING

Networking is just meeting people – either in the real world or online. There's a good definition of it on Entrepreneur.com[8]:

> *"The process of developing and using your contacts to increase your business, enhance your knowledge, expand your sphere of influence, or serve your community."*

Wow, that really takes the pressure off as many authors get quite twitchy about the idea of networking. Sometimes they don't like it because they are a bit shy and dislike the idea of trying to sell themselves or their books.

The idea of merely expanding your contacts and sphere of influence, and enhancing your knowledge is much more appealing.

As an author, networking can help give you credibility, establish your expertise, and raise the profile of your books and yourself. It can make a massive difference to your earning potential and give you terrific contacts who you can learn from. It can be real-world networking but it can also be virtual, online networking, in various forms.

---

[8] http://www.entrepreneur.com/article/225067

Does the idea of networking terrify you or excite you? Many authors are quite daunted by the prospect. Don't worry if you aren't a naturally sociable/outgoing person.

Let's go back to Susan Cain again (the author of *Quiet*). After her childhood experiences of feeling that being introverted was a weakness and made her a failure, she worked hard to try to become an extrovert – or at least to convince others that she was an extrovert:

> *"I became a Wall Street lawyer instead of the writer that I had always longed to be – partly because I needed to prove to myself that I could be bold and assertive.*
>
> *I was always going off to crowded bars when I really would have preferred a quiet dinner with friends. I made these self-negating choices so reflexively that I wasn't even aware that I was making them.*
>
> *This is what many introverts do. It's our loss, for sure, but it's also our colleagues' loss and our communities' loss and – at the risk of sounding grandiose – it's the world's loss. Because when it comes to creativity and to leadership, we need introverts doing what they do best."*
>
> Susan Cain, author of *Quiet: The Power of Introverts In a World That Can't Stop Talking*

Susan Cain defines introversion not as being shy, but being about how you respond to stimulation. Extroverts crave large amounts of stimulation but introverts feel most alive and most capable and switched-on when they are in quieter, more low-key environments.

She says:

> *The key to maximizing our talents is for us all to put ourselves in the zone of stimulation that is right for us.*

That's amazing and useful advice. We don't need to force ourselves into situations that would make us particularly uncomfortable. That would lead us to come across as either a nervous, grumpy wreck, or as false and unauthentic.

> ### HOW NETWORKING AFFECTS YOU:
>
> Networking is important but it doesn't have to be done face-to-face.
>
> The key is not to put on a false cheesy grin and go to a huge writer's conference to do some networking when you'd rather be meditating on top of a mountain.
>
> It's about finding the "zone of stimulation that is right for you", as Susan Cain says in *Quiet*.
>
> Your zone may be:
>
> ➢ Sitting at a computer sending out press releases and accepting an occasional telephone interview with a reporter.
>
> ➢ Writing a few guest posts for blogs.
>
> ➢ Being a guest on some teleseminars or webinars.
>
> ➢ Starting your own blog and inviting others to write guest posts or do interviews with you.
>
> Networking is about meeting people – that can be virtual or physical. It can be at times to suit you and in ways to suit you. Don't feel you have to hide just because you aren't a party animal.

All these things: Marketing/Advertising, Reputation management, Spinning, Sales, Sending loads of press releases, Telephoning reporters, and Networking can come under the umbrella of PR but PR includes more and more tools as we get more digitally-savvy.

Whether you choose to use any or all of these things is up to you and your level of comfort in how you are prepared to put yourself out there.

You will need to use at least some of the main PR tools:

1. Making relationships with and being available for reporters, the public, and your peers via:

   ➢ Press releases – sending to individual reporters/news outlets and distributing online to improve SEO, give backlinks to your website, and boost social proof online.

   ➢ Social media – including the main social media platforms: Twitter, Facebook, Google+, LinkedIn, Pinterest; as well as the main book cataloging sites: Goodreads, Shelfari, LibraryThing; and also your website/blog, other people's blogs.

   ➢ Newsletters – to people who subscribe to your 'list'. Maintaining an ongoing relationship with your list is one of the most powerful things you can do to boost your book sales.

> ➢ Events – such as virtual blog tours, book launch parties, etc. It's important to attend other people's events, as well as your own. Many relationships are made over informal chats when the pressure is off.
> ➢ Speaking engagements – offline in libraries, schools, clubs, bookstores, networking events, publishing events; online on podcasts, teleseminars, webinars, YouTube videos, etc.
> ➢ Advertising – e.g. Facebook or Goodreads ads, paid book placement on book sites, etc.
> ➢ Promotions – competitions of your own, as well as offering a prize in others' competitions.

2. A media kit, consisting of:

> ➢ Your bio.
> ➢ List of FAQ (and answers).
> ➢ A good photograph of you.
> ➢ A list of your books and [possibly] speaking engagements.

Next, we'll look at the skills needed for one of the biggest jobs in PR – writing a press release.

---

*If you enjoyed this excerpt, you can find **PR for Authors** in Kindle and print formats on Amazon.*

ACKNOWLEDGEMENTS

THIS BOOK TOOK MANY months to research, test, implement, write, and update. Special thanks to Kat for her help and support.

Big thanks and mucho appreciation to author and illustrator Neil Groom for the lovely cover for this book.

Huge thanks to International bestselling author and publisher Cheryl Kaye Tardif for her support, encouragement, and endorsement.

Finally, thanks to the rest of my wonderful family for their love and support: Mum, Dad, Josh, Becky, Andrew, and all the animals! X

ABOUT
THE AUTHOR

❧❧

MICHELLE CAMPBELL-SCOTT WAS born Michelle (AKA Mia) Campbell in the maternity unit of a hospital near Liverpool in England during the hey-days of The Beatles. She was a few weeks late and has struggled to catch up ever since.

Although she enjoys visiting Liverpool, she does not consider herself to be a Scouser. She is a Lancastrian, from a village in the Lancashire foothills (Liverpool used to be a Lancashire city until the government changed the boundaries – there were riots about that!).

Her mother is as book-mad as she is. One of Michelle's earliest memories is of her Mom sitting on the floor reading, with a vacuum cleaner next to her. She had spotted an interesting book while cleaning, picked it up, and got engrossed! She also remembers her Dad stepping over a pile of books and saying, "If you love them so much, why don't you try writing one?" She did, and hasn't stopped since.

She is a former teacher who also worked in public relations. She spent a number of years writing freelance, as well as writing and delivering training courses for businesses and on digital platforms. She left teaching in 2012 to write full-time. The dogs are happier now she doesn't go out to work but they do resent the amount of time she spends with the computer. Michelle also writes as Michelle Booth and Mia Campbell.

Her author profiles on Goodreads are:

www.goodreads.com/michellecampbellscott | www.goodreads.com/michellebooth
http://www.goodreads.com/miacampbell

INDEX

❧❧